You

Are

the

Universe

MASAMI SAIONJI

You

Are

the

Universe

ISBN-13: 978-1-4196-7826-4
ISBN-10: 1-4196-7826-4

Translators: Kinuko Hamaya, Seiji Hashimoto, Mary McQuaid

Editors: David W. Edelstein, Annie Wilson, Julie Doxsee, Christopher Bartone

Contents

Preface 7

1 Taking Responsibility for Our Lives 9

2 Invite Happiness with the Law of
   Effect and Cause 24

3 We Live in A World of One 39

4 Guide Yourself to Happiness 50

5 True Forgiveness 66

6 Praise Your Mind 79

7 Declaring the Will of the Universal Law 97

Appendix I
   Fading Away—May Peace Prevail on Earth:
   A Teaching of Absolute Love and Forgiveness 113

Appendix II
   Words of Happiness and Light 115

Appendix III

Gratitude to the World of Nature 118

Appendix IV

Interview with Masami Saionji:

Questions and Answers about the Universal *IN*

for the Self 125

Introducing the Universal *IN* for Humanity 139

Appendix V

How to Form the Universal *IN* for the Self 140

How to Form the Universal *IN* for Humanity 156

Appendix VI

Interview with Masami Saionji:

Questions and Answers about Mandalas 172

Appendix VII

A New, Quick, and Effective Method 192

Notes 194

About the Author 197

Preface

With the passing of the centuries, the memory of their ultimate truth had faded from the hearts of human beings, being supplanted by ignorance and distorted beliefs. Also, the ultimate truth had for a long time been bent, twisted, and covered up by people who feared that it might rob them of their authority.

By 'ultimate truth,' I mean the truth about the hidden identity of each human being. Unseen by most, this truth had continued to twinkle like a universe filled with stars, until it suddenly burst forth again. Like the sea at full tide, the echo of truth rang forcefully, urging us toward our awakening. The pulse of truth beat powerfully. The light of truth flashed through the sky. The words of truth split the darkness: *You are the Universe! The Universe is you! You are Infinity! Infinity is you!*

From the beginning, you have been truth itself, divinity itself. All of humanity, without a single exception, is the very life-power of the limitless universe.

Do you find this hard to believe? Perhaps you think that your eyes and ears are playing tricks on you. Perhaps you are asking yourself: 'How could someone as wretched, untalented, untruthful, impure, lazy, and cowardly as me be one with the infinite, divine power that moves the universe? It's absurd. It can't be true.'

But it *is* true. You really *are* the universe. And the universe is you—the real you.

No matter what kind of situation you might be in, and no matter how forcefully your emotions, miseries, and fears might seem to control you, none of them are you. They have nothing to do with the real you.

As you read this book, I believe that something mysteriously wonderful might happen. One by one, your doubts and confusion might be swept away as you remember the truth that has been concealed within you. You will become conscious of the infinite divine life that flows within you and within all human beings, and you will awaken to an inner certainty that, someday soon, the infiniteness of the universe will be clearly expressed through you.

You are the universe. Each human being is the universe. At long last, we have stepped into an age when humanity can come face to face with this truth.

Masami Saionji
January 1996

CHAPTER 1

Taking Responsibility for Our Lives

Looking at the current world situation, we sense that never before have there been times as chaotic as these. We see civil wars, armed conflicts, terrorism, starvation, accidents and catastrophes. All over the world, *karma*[1] is erupting and sounding an alarm to the human race. And behind it all, the insidious energy of religious and ethnic hostility continues to twist and swirl in intricate patterns, sometimes rising to the surface and sometimes staying hidden from view.

Meanwhile, the vast majority of us keep trying to block these circumstances out of our minds, as if what is happening had nothing to do with our lives now. For a moment, of course, the emerging conflicts and miseries cause us to shudder, and we wish we could shield our eyes from it all. But that feeling quickly degenerates into a stereotyped reaction, and a great many of us, though we do feel sorry for those directly involved, see no connection between those miseries and our own way of living. The only things that really hold our interest are our own personal concerns: our families, our jobs, and our personal aims and wishes.

In reality, though, can the matter be swept aside so easily?

Are conflicts in other regions totally unrelated to our own present lives? I do not believe that they are. It looks very much as if the era is finally drawing near when each individual must seriously come to grips with his or her own personal way of living. If each of us continues to live just as we have been, the Earth will not survive.

Virtually everyone in the world is weak and unstable. The great majority of people are living without really recognizing what it is that they deeply and truly believe in. How is it that people today have managed to somehow get by in this chaotic world, even if our lifestyles are less than ideal? It is because, at some point or other, we have all depended on others.

Because each of us feels so insecure, the mere fact of having our family or friends at our side seems to lighten the burden we feel in having to face life alone. If we just immerse ourselves in our closely-knit family or circle of friends and nestle together, we feel that no need will arise for us to earnestly tackle the question: *What is the purpose of my life?*—a question which lies deeply embedded in our hearts and arises from time to time to reprimand us. Yet as we continue to divert our attention from this question, sooner or later it fades from our minds. And as long as we are never alone, and always have someone at our side, we can enjoy a false sense of reprieve from that oppressive question. So, we continue to make every effort not to be left on our own.

Living as part of a crowd has become a habit. It covers up the need to deeply reflect on our state of mind and to scrutinize our innermost heart. Choosing instead to fill our lives with the sharing of joys, sorrows, and hardships proves to be far more reassuring.

Rather than deeply pondering our lives and constructing

our futures creatively, most of us prefer things the other way round. We like to base our actions on what we see around us, never departing from our fixed pattern. We adjust our way of life to what others say and do.

It is, of course, wonderful to move forward and elevate ourselves by supporting each other and joining hands together. However, before humanity can truly join closely together, each individual must build a firm sense of his or her essential purpose in this world.

The weakest point in human beings' thinking is the notion that we can develop our own lives while at the same time relying on others, humoring others, and courting the favor of others. This thought is what keeps us forever unable to draw out our own true personalities and beliefs.

As a result, we feel too insecure to move ahead with our lives on our own. When something comes up, we are unable to solve the problem by ourselves. We keep our eyes on those around us, and by mimicking what others think or do, we end up repeating the same patterns again and again. This somehow makes us feel secure. If things do not work out well, we content ourselves with the thought that similar woes are shared by others. This provides a sense of relief, and we question the matter no further.

Who am I? What am I living for? Questions like these, which pertain to the way a human being is meant to live, must be asked by each and every one of us. Yet, when we run into these questions, most of us just look around and notice that no one else seems to be tackling the problem in earnest. And so, although the problem continues to trouble us, we end up suppressing it. Affecting an air of composure, we glance around us, assume a pleased expression and a happy-go-lucky attitude, and this makes us feel reassured.

❧ *Taking the Easy Way Out*

The long and the short of it is that we human beings do not feel confident enough to make our own decisions—even about our own personal matters. A superficial glance might give us the illusion that we are reaching all our decisions on our own, but it is not so. Rather, we continually rely on the guidance, advice, and orders that are forthcoming from those around us. For almost everyone, making no decisions on our own is by far the easiest way to live. All we have to do is simply comply with the directives given by others—wives, husbands, friends, teachers, society, and so on. Taking our cues from others has become the most basic pattern for conducting life in today's world. And it is precisely because people have lived according to the will of others that an orderly society has emerged.

Living in obedience to this system is a very deeply rooted custom, not easily overturned by the power of one individual. Even when having to take orders gives rise to discontent and resentment, it still remains distinctly easier than having to make one's decisions for oneself. As a result, we see people everywhere leading a life of conformity. And since everyone else is living that way, it seems only natural to each of us that we should do the same.

Yet, absolute authority over others has never been ordained to anyone by God. Nor is there a divine dictate as to how we are to live our lives. All such systems are of human making. Religious and educational systems, ethics, laws, and penalties—all these have been created by humanity. The thought has taken root in our minds that these systems have a power exceeding that of an individual. Yet in reality, humanity has no need at all to adjust to any system, much less obey it.

At present, the intrinsic personality of each individual has not yet been fully brought out, nor do we have an understanding of our essential purpose in life. Such being the case, it is no wonder that we find it far simpler to subordinate ourselves to an outside power, and take orders from others, than to seriously consider our own duties and responsibilities as an individual. In opting for the easy way, we do not have to tax our brain pondering difficult philosophies. We do not have to assess our personal life with regard to spiritual principles. All we have to do is be attentive to the expectations of the people around us, and behave just as they do. In following this route, no mistakes are made and no problems arise.

I think we could say that the reason why nations have established themselves in the form that we see today, and are able to carry out their practices and policies, is that all of us have been following orders and living in compliance with the will of others. I think we could say that the reason why despotism still reigns in many parts of the world is that individuals have not awakened to their inner truth, and do not clearly discern what it is that they truly believe in. Even if some may have identified their true beliefs, most of these people are still behaving timidly and lack the courage to convert their beliefs into action.

If we could go to the roots of wars, ethnic and religious conflicts, disease, starvation, and so on, I think we would find that the cause lies with each individual person. From now on, if each of us does not hold firmly to the beliefs that rise from the innermost depths of our being, there is a great danger that our ability to distinguish bad from good may become utterly lost.

❧ The Pitfall of Obedience

For example, if we look back on the days of the Second World War and the genocide of the Jewish people, what we come face to face with is the mentality of each individual human being. The killings that took place could not possibly have been perpetrated through the absolute power of a handful of people. One look at the scale of what happened should make it clear that many thousands participated in it, or were somehow involved. There were those who caught and arrested each person; there were those who prosecuted them, guarded them, confirmed their gender and age, sent them into the gas chambers, switched on the gas, disposed of the corpses, and so on. There were a great, great many people who took part in it, all in the name of obedience.

Yet this does not mean that all those who participated were unparalleled in their cruelty and cold-bloodedness. They were not. In terms of their individual lifestyles, most were considerate, affectionate, reasonable people who would never entertain thoughts of killing others. They were circumspect, law-abiding citizens. However, when it came to state orders, or orders from their superiors, those modest citizens were transformed in an instant. In the name of obedience, they began behaving in a way that defies the imagination. When ordered to kill their fellow human beings, they firmly believed that it was their duty to do so.

If people are ordered to commit acts that go against their conscience, they face the ethical responsibility of deciding, as individuals, whether or not to obey those orders. Yet when such a situation arises, many find themselves unable to accept this responsibility, and they cannot make the crucial decision on their own. And so, hiding behind the excuse of obedience, they drive the voice of their conscience into the recesses of their hearts. Then they make various excuses to themselves, justifying their inability to stand up to authority.

Many find that obeying orders gives them such a sense of purpose that it overshadows any other feelings—whether defiance, or reluctance, or love, or shame. This is the stance taken by a majority of human beings. They are not wicked, nor are they cruel or immoral. Just like you and me, they are people richly endowed with common sense. They are people who shed real blood and weep real tears—civic-minded, well-intentioned people. Personally, they do not feel that what they are doing is actually good, but they steadfastly believe it is their duty to follow the orders given to them.

In thinking this way, they are firmly convinced that the actions they take under orders are not their own responsibility. Even if they have killed thousands or tens of thousands of innocent people, it does not occur to them that their actions are their own responsibility. What a formidable thought that is! They have killed, yet they think that they have not sinned. They believe that the sin belongs to another, that the responsibility lies with those who issued the order to kill. Again and again, they try to vindicate themselves by explaining that they had no choice in the matter, that they were acting against their own wishes, under the orders received. This loss of a personal sense of responsibility, under the guise of obedience to absolute authority, is the most dangerous pitfall that threatens the future of human beings.

Nowadays, too, mass killings are taking place all over the world in the name of the nation, or the ethnic group, or the religion. This is not someone else's concern. Without a doubt, the time will come when each of us will face a similar situation.

To Steadily Face Our Own Life

If you or I were left completely alone, would we be able to look straight into our life and face it without fear, calmly grasping the reality of it? Suppose that, due to an earthquake, for example, you were locked in an elevator and left on your own for hours or even days. What would you do? Suppose that you were left utterly alone in complete darkness, with not a soul around to answer your cries. What would you do? Or, suppose that you were left completely alone on an isolated island and were obliged to go on living there. What would you do? Would you fall prey to fear, or would you calmly seek your way from within?

Up to now, the great majority of us have been totally uninterested in this kind of question. We have thought that such situations are quite unusual, and happen only to certain unlucky people—never to us.

But is that correct? Is there no need to reflect upon such a possibility? Up to now, someone has always been near at hand. Even a person who lives alone can normally find someone else nearby. For almost all of us, facing life completely on our own is out of the question. And until now, humanity has been able to survive fairly well with this way of thinking. However, we can conceive of a very different kind of world—a world that is gradually taking shape and is starting to emerge even now. If human beings do not soon learn how to truly face themselves, they might easily become lost in that world.

In the new world that is taking shape, everything will move with tremendous velocity. All travel—by land, air, or sea—will enter an era of super-speed. In all fields, computers and machinery will take over the work of human beings. Surrounded by an intricate network of information media, the individual will no longer have to distinguish good from bad with his or her own thought processes.

More and more, each person will be of the same mold. Those who give serious thought to various matters will be nowhere to be found. All around us, everyone will be fed the same, one-sided information, and the whole of society will express exactly the same reaction to it. There will be no point at all in expressing personal ideas or opinions. Radio, television, and newspapers will inundate all citizens with identical thoughts and information, and individuals will cease airing their differing reactions to it.

Top-ranking commentators will present their comments; scientists will offer their criticism; educators will give direction; religious leaders will provide guidance. All answers will convey the same point of view. The process of reaching a conclusion after deeply pondering a question will be eliminated. Only the conclusion will be offered. All that we human beings will have to do is to act in accordance with the information provided.

All fields will become more and more specialized, and since suitable experts will supply us with their wholly specialized knowledge, there will be no room left for us to wedge in an opinion. We will believe ourselves to be no match for the experts, no matter how we may strive and exert ourselves. The only way left open to us will be to accept and believe all the expert knowledge given to us, swallowing it whole. Be it matters of law, politics, religion, psychology, health, childcare, or falling in love, we will be wholly convinced that we cannot hold a candle to the experts who have specialized in those fields.

Since personal ideas and opinions will have lost all function, the information media will let flow a stream of specialized knowledge and superlative solutions. Our one and only option will be to absorb it and put it into practice. No one will have any means of judging whether it corresponds with truth[2] or not. By that time, people will have lost even their faculty for questioning things, or noting when they do not ring true. All people will behave with complete uniformity, as if hypnotized. Our only course of action will be to preserve the status quo.

In a materially-oriented society, once things start to move at tremendous speed, everything becomes mechanized and specialized. We can find no one at all who is able to perceive what it is to be a total human being. More and more, people are viewed in material terms. Matters relating to the mind and spirit are abandoned. Human beings continue to drift farther and farther from their divinity, separating themselves from truth.

In that kind of world, the functions of the mind and spirit are no longer thought necessary. The aching of the heart is ignored. Since all matters are regulated by machines and resolved in material terms only, the emotions are disregarded. This can result only in self-destruction. The various inventions and discoveries that were intended to serve the common good will have turned into the instruments of our own ruin.

One such trend that has already taken its toll on human beings is the over-development of medical technology. Instead of enhancing the public welfare, as we hoped they would, new techniques and machinery often restrict our lives and cause us greater confusion. No one seems able to put a stop to it.

Throwing ethics, conscience, and common sense to the wind, humanity is rushing straight ahead at breakneck speed along an extremely dangerous road.

Time to Align Ourselves with Truth

Meanwhile, our divine consciousness is hard at work, trying to jolt us into an awakening. Unfortunately though, humanity has already drifted so far from its original truth that it is next to impossible for the majority of people to change their direction all at once, no matter how intelligent they might be. And so, starting with just one person, then two, then three, then ten, then a thousand, individuals are striving to make a difference by attuning themselves to their inner truth. In doing so, they hope that their physical selves may serve as instruments, or 'vessels,' for sending harmonious energy throughout the Earth.

The pure, ultimate energy of the universe needs workplaces, or vessels, for healing the Earth and promoting the evolution of humanity. When I say 'workplace' or 'vessel,' I mean that it is necessary for universal, divine energy to work through a physical or material entity. However bright and powerful it may be, this universal energy cannot be brought down and spread through humanity if there are no people or places that serve as intermediary vessels for receiving it. The existence of such vessels is utterly indispensable. Without such vessels, or workplaces, it becomes impossible for the laws of harmony to manifest themselves on Earth.

In the ancient past, people had a firm grasp of this truth, and they built churches, temples, and shrines in many places,. allowing divine functions to descend to Earth there. People then gathered at such sites to pray and to keep those places attuned to God.

Infinite, divine wisdom can descend to Earth at purified places, and also through the intermediary bodies of individual human beings. These persons are described as 'awakened ones' or 'divine incarnations.' Holy ones such as Sakyamuni Buddha,[3] Jesus, Mohammed, and other saints and wise people who have left their imprint on history have all brought the ultimate energy of the universe down to Earth by letting their physical selves serve as divine vessels.

There is a wide range of people of varying levels who act as 'intermediary vessels.' Some have awakened to their divine reality and bring the sublime truth—the absolute laws of the universe—down to Earth. Apart from these holy ones, there is another category of vessels: people who give guidance on matters relating to material profit, and call their teachings 'divine messages.' These people are indeed vessels, but of a different sort. They receive vibrations from low-level, unharmonious souls, and are prone to being controlled by them. Vessels who serve as bases for these sorts of unawakened beings have the following things in common: they have deeply-rooted selfish desires, and are very adept at finding out where their advantages and disadvantages lie. They think only of themselves, and their lifestyles are very far removed from truth. Vessels who are utilized by low-level souls are a source of confusion for humanity. They disturb the public order, violate the laws of harmony, and continue to inundate human beings with waves of unharmonious thought-energy.

In summary, to flow through this three-dimensional, physical world, the power, functions, and energy of other-dimensional realms require vessels who can serve as links between those realms and this physical one.

The laws of harmony are always radiating infinite light, infinite abundance, and infinite wisdom to our world. But this power, this light, this energy, wisdom, and love can only become manifest through an intermediary base or workplace. Above all, the laws of harmony need to work through people who have awakened to truth. By working through these splendid vessels, universal divine wisdom can assist this world in averting disaster and shifting its course toward harmony.

Unless one's physical being is shining, one cannot become a superlative vessel for receiving and transmitting the brilliant energy of the universe. A physical being that is heavily soiled with greedy thoughts and feelings cannot act as a vessel for universal truth. The reason for this is that such people are extremely susceptible to the control of unharmonious forces, and can easily end up falling prey to them.

In the years ahead, the universal law needs to work though more and more vessels who have awakened to their inner divine truth. Through these vessels, the harmonizing energy of the universe will be able to connect with humanity and spread out widely. And as more and more people devote themselves to that aim, the spirit of love and harmony can manifest itself more and more fully.

❧ A Personal Note

A few years ago, my work entered a new phase when I spent two years overseas, with the aim of devoting myself to intensive prayers for eight hours each day. During those daily prayers, this one physical body of mine was entrusted with tasks in a variety of different fields.

One of those tasks was to emit purifying energy to the ethnic conflicts, abnormal weather conditions, environmental destruction, and other sufferings that were occurring across the globe. Through prayer, my physical entity served as a vessel for manifesting, on this earthly plane, universal energy aimed at awakening humanity to its intrinsic identity. Also, during these prayers, a number of new *INs*[4] were delivered to Earth in rapid succession. I was also entrusted with the mission of receiving principles of cosmic science[5] from the universal law for the benefit of humanity. In addition, it was necessary for me to reason with, guide, and purify confused souls whose turbulent emotions confined them to the lower subconscious worlds and worlds of lightlessness. There were times, too, when I prayed nonstop for the people in a particular country that was steeped in crisis. In ways like these, I assumed a number of diverse functions by means of this one physical body.

The universal wisdom has worked out truly far-reaching plans for uplifting humanity from its current disharmony, and there are a number of methods available to people who wish to assist in this process. I would like to acquaint my readers with some of the methods which I have found to be highly effective in promoting the happiness of individuals and, at the same time, of the Earth and humanity as a whole. These practices are (1) praying for world peace, (2) filling our minds with only bright words and thoughts, (3) living with gratitude to nature, (4) performing the universal *INs*, (5) creating living *mandalas*, and (6) practicing a simple spiritual breathing method. To learn more about these practices, please see the appendices to this book.

❧ *The Years Ahead of Us*

In devoting ourselves to practices like these, step by step, we can awaken ourselves to our inner truth. No matter how rapidly humanity keeps rushing blindly ahead, no matter to what degree it becomes mechanized, over-specialized, and increasingly materially-minded, we ourselves will not lose our universal perspective. We are overflowing with hope and confidence, and are enlivened by a sense of certainty that, as long as we remain on this Earth, its destruction can still be averted.

The years just ahead of us will be of great significance. Now is the time for us all to truly know ourselves and awaken to our own, original purpose.

It is a stern, unrelenting reality and there is no easy way to say it: now, at long last, the time is drawing near when each of us must take responsibility for our own actions. Each of us, individually, will have to comprehend the extent to which our way of living has strayed from our original truth.

Everyone, let us devote ourselves in all sincerity to returning to our original spirit of harmony, so that all of us can live freely and happily in the world of the twenty-first century.

You are the Universe

First published in December 1993

CHAPTER 2

Invite Happiness with the Law of Effect and Cause

Which came first, the chicken or the egg? Everyone has heard this age-old question, and we could debate it at great length without ever finding an answer.

Let us suppose that the egg existed first, and later became a hen. We are then left with the riddle of where the egg came from in the first place. Inevitably, we have to conclude that the egg was born of the hen. The hen, however, was born from the egg. The cycle of cause and effect continues endlessly, and no one knows where it truly begins or ends.

For the moment, let us define the egg as the cause and the hen as the effect. One person might say that the cause (the egg) came first, while another might say that the effect (the hen) preceded the cause. Neither party could say that the other was wrong. Depending on your outlook and way of thinking, you could subscribe either to the law of *cause and effect* or to the law of *effect and cause*. It seems to me that everyone is entirely free to choose from either of them.

At this point, you might be saying that you know about the law of cause and effect, but have never heard of the law of effect and cause. That is because the law of effect and cause is a new term, which I have created. Under the law of *cause and effect*, there is first a cause, which is followed by an effect. With the law of *effect and cause*, there is first an effect, which in turn produces a new cause.

What is my reason for introducing this concept? For a long time, people have been suffering under the restrictions of their own inflexible ideas, unable to set themselves free. It pains my heart to see their anguish, and I would like to assist them in rising above it. I strongly wish to help people extricate themselves from those self-created fetters, so that they can live happier and more creative lives.

The Law of Cause and Effect

If you sow violet seeds in the ground, violets will grow and bloom. Here, the planting of the seeds is the cause. It precedes its effect, the blooming of violets.

'Because the couple fell in love, they married'...'Because the mother-in-law always bullied her daughter-in-law, the daughter-in-law came to dislike her'...'Because the husband was unfaithful, the marriage ended in divorce.' In these examples, we again recognize certain causes as producing certain effects.

All the various circumstances in the world can be explained through this principle of cause and effect. Where there is no cause, there can be no effect. Effects are produced precisely because there are causes. This principle is widely known in this world and is accepted as a natural law.

Yet if they thoroughly understand this law, why do people keep repeating the same mistakes over and over again? If they recognize that their present pain and sadness are the results of past causes, why do they not vow never again to repeat those same failures? Seeming none the wiser, why do they newly sow the very same seeds of misery? When we see this happening again and again, it makes us wonder about the usefulness of the law of cause and effect.

Certainly, we can say that our fate in this world takes shape through a series of causes and effects. Behind each sorrow, behind each war, behind each instance of starvation, illness, and disaster, there is a cause somewhere in the past. One by one, each individual has sown the seeds of all sorts of misery and pain. Their effects can be seen and felt in today's world. Because human beings are not truly aware of this, they continue to focus their energy on creating new causes that bring more and more misery and distress.

The seeds, or causes, that are sown by an individual can naturally be expected to produce effects at some point in that person's future. And it goes without saying that they also influence the nation, the ethnic group, and the various other groups and organizations to which the person belongs. We must never forget that a nation is made up of all its individual citizens, just as any group is the product of all its members.

That is why it is so important for every single member of the human race to pay close attention to what is happening when they create the causes of their future conditions. If everyone in the world were to refrain from creating the causes of misery, illness, war, and disharmony, the future of humanity would naturally take a turn for the better.

Every moment gives rise to a new cause. Let us not spend each new moment creating negative causes by constantly sowing the seeds of unhappiness. The choice is entirely up to us. We need to be fully conscious of our own thoughts and actions, recognizing and avoiding those that might cause future misery.

As we develop this kind of awareness, we come to see that we have been the ones responsible for our own feelings of distress, and we will no longer blame others for our unhappiness. Up until now, we may have felt that our problems were the fault of the nation, the government, our neighbors, our spouse or partner, or our relatives. We may have been unaware of what we ourselves were doing. If we had clearly and correctly assessed our own thoughts and actions, we would not have experienced our present unhappiness, as its cause would not have been created.

The law of cause and effect offers us a great key for identifying the source of our unhappiness. But in actual practice, it is extremely difficult to use this law for the improvement of our fate.

❧ Invite Happiness with the Law of Effect and Cause

The law of effect and cause, however, fully transcends the law of cause and effect.

Let us consider an example. A person feels that if he had a large amount of money, he would be happy. Viewed in terms of the law of cause and effect, the possession of money is the cause, and happiness is the effect. The only drawback is that money is a finite commodity in this world. If a minority of wealthy people were to gather up a huge proportion of the world's money, the amount remaining for other people would naturally decrease. Consequently, although each person might yearn for money, affluence would not come to all of us. If happiness is indeed measured in terms of how much money we have, some of us are bound to be unhappy because we have too little of it.

Under the law of cause and effect, the cause of unhappiness always stems from the finite world. For example, people tend to think: 'If only I had assets!' 'If only I had a house, or land!' 'If only I were more beautiful, or had a better figure, or a better physique!' 'If only I were younger!' 'If only I had better academic credentials, or worked for a more prestigious company, or came from a better background!' There is no end to the list of things that people yearn for. When we confine our thinking to the finite, material world, it is inevitable that some of us will find happiness while others are relegated to unhappy situations.

The law of effect and cause, however, begins where we transcend the causes of the material world. The principle is that we first generate an effect, so that a new cause naturally follows. We call forth an effect that already exists deep within our being. Rather than focusing on what is finite, we turn our attention to what is infinite. We focus on the limitless qualities in the realm of the spirit.

Actually, it is much easier to start by generating the effect in advance of the cause. This is because the effect already exists within us. Infinite love, infinite health, infinite flourishing, infinite happiness, infinite joy, infinite life, infinite abundance: all these are aspects of the absolute reality existing within each human heart. When we attune our consciousness to these infinite qualities, they will spontaneously generate their own new causes.

Happiness is first awakened in the heart. Then, by the functioning of the energy called forth from the heart, everything that causes happiness will be drawn toward us. Even material happiness and happy human relationships will spontaneously begin heading in our direction. A harmonious partner or spouse and harmonious relatives will appear in front of us, just as we expected—and their appearance marks the birth of a new cause.

When we live according to this principle, we recognize that the 'effect' exists in the limitless realm of our spirit. An infinitely flourishing future already resides within us. Infinite harmony already fills our mind. Whenever we exert our own, infinitely abundant creativity, a new cause will always follow.

This is the point I would like to emphasize: never be captivated by the causes belonging to the material world. When you direct your attention to the world of the infinite, the world of the spirit, the phenomena that you desire will naturally take shape in your life. Rather than limiting your happiness to the quantity of your material benefits, remember that everything you desire already exists in a world far surpassing the material one.

Try thinking of the already happy person who exists within you. Let yourself imagine a feeling of continual harmony, calm, and peace of mind. Believe in the *you* who joins hands with others, sharing a life of mutual help and encouragement. Envision a joyful family where you are surrounded by your wonderful spouse or partner and wonderful children. Picture yourself as you truly are in essence: radiant with health and vitality, living in harmony with the universe.

If you are always at one with the universe, how can the causes of unhappiness ever affect you? If your heart always lives in a shining world, there is no way for suffering, anguish, or sorrow to arise. All these bright 'effects' are inherent in your true self. They exist within you. It is important for all of us to know this well, and remember it.

❧ *Release the Karmic Causes of the Past*

How pointless it is to live in constant fear of the law of cause and effect. Once a seed has been sown, we cannot remedy the situation by worrying about it. If we always live dreading the effects of our past actions, we will spend our days in apprehension and fear.

When the effects of your past actions emerge in your life, you must firmly believe that all those things are appearing now in order to vanish forever. Do not be hampered or distracted by those vanishing traces of the past. Continue to live brightly and confidently, in the firm belief that when those past causes have disappeared, things will absolutely get better.

My explanation of effect and cause is a philosophy of steadfast, light-oriented thinking. It offers a method for focusing our thoughts only on the light—a way to call forth our unlimited potential and attune our minds to what is infinite. Its purpose is to allow each of us to approach closer and closer to our intrinsic, complete self, and to give expression to that self.

At the same time, it is truly a simple method to follow. When a dark thought crosses your mind, counter it with a bright thought such as 'I am light!' Whenever a pessimistic feeling surrounds you, pierce through it with the positive energy of words like 'Infinite improvement!' From morning till night, as much as you can, create shining new causes with thoughts like 'I am love! I am harmony! Infinite power! May peace prevail on Earth!'[6]

If, instead, you become engrossed in tracking down the causes of each and every occurrence in your life, or each and every problem in the world, and try to analyze them according to the law of cause and effect, your efforts may never reach a conclusion.

Here is just one example of where a purely causative approach can lead us. A man is not happy (effect). Why is he not happy? As a child, he was not loved by his mother (cause). Here we see the functioning of the law of cause and effect.

Next, we ask why he was not loved (effect). It was because he was a rebellious child (cause). Why was he rebellious (effect)? It was because his mother ignored him in favor of her other children (cause). Why did his mother ignore him while showering affection on her other children (effect)? It was because, unlike her other children, he had a gloomy disposition (cause). Why was he gloomy as a child (effect)? It was because he was not given the things he wished for (cause). Why was he not given the things he wished for (effect)? It was because his family was short of funds (cause). Why was his family short of funds (effect)? And so on.

As we can see from this one example, tracking down the causes of our circumstances is a never-ending process. Furthermore, we can never clearly identify one single cause for an occurrence. There are always many overlapping causes behind it. However far back we might go, we can never clearly pinpoint any one single cause.

If we traced the matter back to the person's infancy, and tried to discover why he was born in those circumstances, we would have to trace his existence even further back, to a time before he was born in this world. But even if we were able to do so, we would not be able to isolate any one single cause. And when it comes to analyzing the conditions among groups of people, societies, and nations, the causes become even more complex. Behind every world problem, there is an interweaving of historical, cultural, social, economic, and emotional factors at work.

This is why I say that it is no simple matter to live by a cause-and-effect philosophy. It is not a question of one single cause bringing about one single effect. If you endlessly search through the past for the causes of your unhappiness, or for the causes behind the world's problems, you may be heading deeper into an ever-expanding labyrinth of confusion. And ultimately, unless you can clearly identify the original and most fundamental cause, your efforts will not be truly meaningful.

Let us say that, within a limited context, you succeed in rooting out the cause you were looking for, and the situation seems to have improved as a result. Later on, however, a somewhat similar circumstance occurs. Why does it occur? It occurs because the cause you once identified is not the fundamental one. It was merely one link in an endless chain. That is why nothing has changed fundamentally.

How can we change things in a fundamental way? We must do more than simply change outward conditions or dispel external causes. The important thing is to make a change within ourselves, to make a change in our thinking. Though we might try to be happy or healthy, or to live a harmonious life, that alone may not be enough. Unless we transform all our thoughts to waves of light, and let those luminous thoughts find expression in our daily life, our present circumstances will not change fundamentally. For real change to occur, we must awaken to our true human identity as infinite divine beings, and live our lives as such.

If we really wish to be happy, if we really wish to be healthy and successful, the way to do it is to constantly focus our thoughts, starting this very moment, on the qualities we wish to draw out: infinite happiness, infinite health, infinite harmony, infinite abundance, and infinite success.

Focus on Your True Identity

Our human consciousness is so complex that most of us do not even understand ourselves. How, then, can we be expected to fathom the true identities of our partner or spouse, our children, and others in our lives? In this situation, we simply continue to interact with one another in a confused, unharmonious manner.

At some point in the history of humanity, human beings diverged from the truth. We shut out the memory of our original, shining identity. We lost our original sense of harmony and oneness with others. Because of this, we had to create rules to help us function smoothly in this world. We created artificial guidelines and ethical systems for the purpose of peacefully interacting with one another. We devised rules to regulate and control each other's behavior, and mold it within the framework of those rules. This led to all sorts of afflictions. After all, people cannot live happily when they are controlled by others or bound by rules. Since humans are, by nature, free beings, we find it unendurable to live a restricted lifestyle. This is why, however fine and good a rule might appear to be, there will always be some who cannot follow it or want to violate it.

The law of cause and effect might also be described as one of the rules that emerged during the long history of human beings' existence. We might indeed say that the law has served to curb people's anti-social behavior. Yet on the other hand, there is no denying that many have suffered from it.

The more conscientious people are, the more likely they are to be inhibited by the law of cause and effect. Some good people are so obsessed with causes and effects that others cannot help wondering why they find it necessary to blame and judge themselves so extensively. The law of cause and effect, which should be leading people to happiness, often has the reverse effect, driving good people away from the light instead of bringing them towards it.

The law of cause and effect may work as an effective deterrent for those who are described as malevolent or unscrupulous people. For well-meaning, conscientious people, though, I feel that the principle of effect and cause is more useful and more natural. While the law of cause and effect functions within the narrow scope of the finite world, the law of effect and cause extends far beyond it, reaching the infinite realm of the true, universal self.

The law of cause and effect emerges from a view of human beings as 'children of sin,' while the law of effect and cause comes from the view that people are children of God. Seeing people as 'children of sin' cannot rescue them from their miseries. True deliverance, I feel, comes only through a concept of human beings as children of God.

If human beings were truly the offspring of sin, our existence could never rise above a guilt-oriented consciousness. Whatever good things we might do, and however we might exert ourselves on behalf of humanity, we would be forever unable to attain true joy, happiness, and freedom. Whenever we returned to the fundamental question of our own human origin, we would again find ourselves locked within a narrow world of hopeless resignation.

The principle that I uphold is that human beings are children of the infinite, divine universe, and are originally formed of light and light alone. If you accept this principle, it naturally follows that everything you need exists within your infinitely brilliant inner light. Consequently, however hard and painful your present experience might be, you will definitely rise above it someday. As soon as you awaken to your true identity as an infinite, universal being, your original nature will be able to manifest itself through your physical existence.

Infinite happiness, infinite provision, and infinite flourishing—all these are included in your original being. Your true self can only live brightly and exuberantly. Your true self can only be happy, healthy, and alive with energy. You are originally filled with deep and abundant love, warmth and compassion. Your true self is by nature perfectly free, and knows no such word as 'impossible.' This is who you really are. This is the real you and the real me.

If your present situation is one of pain, anguish, injury, illness, or frustration, it is not a reflection of your true self. If you fix your attention on your present situation, saying that you are unhappy, that your life is hell, that you want to die, you will be unable to move forward. Before doing that, before doing anything, you must first concentrate on freeing yourself from negative thought habits as quickly as possible. To do this, you must thoroughly and completely transform all your thoughts into bright ones. And for that, the first step is to awaken to your true identity.

Continually remind yourself that you are a brilliantly shining light, an infinite being. Ask yourself if it makes sense for an infinite being to suffer. Ask yourself if it makes sense for there to be anything beyond the comprehension of an infinite being. Ask yourself if it makes sense for an infinite being to believe in the pain of illness. In this way, make up your mind to transform all your thoughts to bright waves of light alone.

Up until now, nearly all of your consciousness may have been oriented toward thoughts of pain, sorrow, inadequacy, and unhappiness. But you can completely reorient your thinking so that it is entirely attuned to the infinite divine light, love, and power of the great Universe. As you get into the habit of doing this, you will gradually be freed from the fixed notions that pervade your subconscious. Step by step, those preconceived, restrictive notions buried deep in the recesses of your mind will be dispelled and purified. Step by step, you will be spontaneously enlivened and guided forward by the bright, positive energy surging forth from within you. The elements that constitute a bright lifestyle will naturally be drawn toward you, and they will take shape in your future.

The Recovery of Lost Intuition

Every day, as I observe the web of confusion in people's hearts, I long to help disentangle it as much as I can. This is why I urge all people to rediscover their forgotten truth at the earliest possible moment.

Strangely enough, the moment of awakening occurs unexpectedly, in the space of an instant. True awakening is not the product of long-term effort, patience, or study, nor does it come with acquired knowledge. As long as you try to discover it with knowledge, it will stay out of your reach.

What is true awakening? True awakening is the recovery of lost intuition—the intuition originally given to each human being. Intuition is the plane through which the light of universal wisdom flows freely into our consciousness. It is because they are merely using their limited material knowledge, instead of tapping into their wondrous, innate intuition, that people continue to wander unnecessarily, shouldering needless burdens and suffering needless worries and afflictions.

Your own intuitive perception is crystal clear. Now, at this moment, attune your heart to your flawless intuition, which comprehends everything. Right now, it can sense what you must do, what you need, and where to direct your steps as you walk along today's path.

Even if you could call forth every particle of knowledge that you have ever acquired, it would not enable you to resolve the difficulties that presently stand before you. However considerable it might be, your knowledge pertains to your past experiences. It does not pertain to the 'you' who exists today. It cannot point out your true direction for the future. While it might perhaps provide assistance in a minor way, it cannot offer you a fundamental solution.

From ancient times until today, how many people have lived out their lives relying only on accumulated knowledge? What legacy has it left us with? The answer is plain for anyone to see. It has given us war after war and illness after illness. It has given us famines, disasters, and all manner of suffering.

At long last, we have come to the moment when each member of humanity must compose his or her thoughts and take a serious look at what has been happening. It is now time for this world to make the transition from our present, material culture to the culture of the future—a bright, flourishing, spiritual culture founded on principles of infinite light and harmony.

Whatever happens, and whatever conflicting emotions may pass through our minds, let's continue to think and speak words that invite happiness and harmony. As a result, even though our consciousness may not always be attuned to our true, universal self, we will see an enormous change from our past mentality, when most of our thoughts were focused on a belief in suffering and misery. Step by step, our bright thoughts will have the effect of creating new causes that give rise to luminous future conditions. The happy situations that we desire will naturally take shape around us, and the wonderful people, things, talents, and insights that we desire will naturally find their way to us.

As more and more of us continue living in this way, with a pure and simple belief in its effectiveness, before long we will discover that we have undergone a marvelous inner transformation. By producing this change in ourselves, we will, at the same time, bring about positive changes in the world.

You are the Universe.

First published in April 1992

CHAPTER 3

We Live in
a World of One

We have recently stepped into the twenty-first century. How can we best live in the society of the future, and how can we prepare for it?

Some might wonder if we human beings will be able to survive on Earth much longer. Some even expect that an entirely new race of people may suddenly appear and carry on in our place. But I do not believe that this will happen. As I see it, that would not be in the natural order of things. Rather, the human beings who live on Earth must evolve with the Earth into the future. It would be unthinkable for us to accept the demise of humanity.

How, then, is humanity to proceed? How can we create a brighter way of life in the years ahead? Although each human being is responsible for answering this urgent question, I feel that most of us have no idea what we should do.

One good look at our current world situation should tell us that, since ages past, there has been no fundamental change in human hearts. On the other hand, there have been extreme changes in our environment. The Earth is in a most critical state, with glaring problems such as environmental deterioration, various forms of pollution, the breakdown of the ozone layer, and dramatic changes in climate.

How can humanity transform itself during the years ahead? As I see it, there is only one answer—we must discover our essential truth and express that truth in our thoughts, words and actions. The truth of our human identity must spread throughout the world.

A Mystical Transformation

The transformation of humanity has already begun. A few years ago, at a sacred spot near Mt. Fuji, some ten or twelve thousand people had a glimpse of the world of the future, the world of truth.[7] Culminating hundreds upon thousands of lifetimes, their eyes were opened for an instant, right here in this world. A ray of radiant, fundamental light was conveyed to them, filling their bodies with wisdom from the universal source.

During that one brief instant, a mystical change took place. Time focused itself on one point, achieving what could not have been done in a thousand or even ten thousand years. For an instant, the flow of time stood still. Then, like a bolt of lightning, the light of truth flashed through the great sky, clearly revealing itself before our eyes. At that instant, the true world came alive in front of the ten or twelve thousand people present.

After the means for humanity's transformation was revealed to us,[8] within a moment the land had resumed its deep tranquility and was returned to the world of the present. Yet during that one instant, ten or twelve thousand people had been showered with the light of truth. Once they had experienced this historical moment, it was remembered in their souls. And so, after returning to the everyday world, even without thinking about it they spontaneously felt an inner longing to continuously speak, think, and act according to their inner, divine truth.

What they experienced could be described as a miraculous event that urged the awakening of humanity through the vessels of those present, for the world of truth actually exists in every human being. Each of those people became conscious of that true world, holding a hidden reservoir of marvelous treasures.

From that moment forward, their lives were transformed. If the changes are not yet apparent to others, this simply means that others have not noticed them. From one instant to the next, those people are changing. Though the changes may still seem indistinct, and their radiance may shine only dimly, the transformation is nothing short of amazing.

As more and more people come to manifest their infinite selves, each of them will become a power source for humanity, and a guide toward the future. Many such people's inner potential is already starting to blossom. In their jobs, their relationships, and all aspects of their lives, their shining existence is starting to be felt by others.

As your infinite, divine self begins to emerge, the atmosphere around you changes, purifying the hearts of others. Your emotions become composed, and you produce a warm-hearted, harmonious feeling in others. In breathing the same air as you do, other people begin to sense changes in themselves. They begin awakening to their own divine truth.

When your infinite self finds expression in this world, it means that the universal will is active where you are. Your existence serves to wonderfully heighten and illuminate the spirits of everyone.

If an increasing number of people were not giving expression to their intrinsic selves, humanity would already have plunged itself into worse agonies than this world has seen so far. The souls of humanity have become so permeated with negative energy that most of us have become wholly indifferent to spiritual truths. With numbed senses, we consume everything, driven by our ravenous material desires. We have become anesthetized to war, to violence, to fear, and to suffering. So deep does the poison in our souls run, one might easily wonder if there is any cure for it. There is so much fear and unrest, illness and starvation, loneliness and alienation in this world that such things are accepted without question as being a natural part of the human condition. This, in itself, is clear testimony to the fact that humanity has lost sight of its original, divine truth.

Human beings today have lost a sense of our own reality. Instead of seeking the vast, spectacular world within us, we seek our identities from other people and other things. Yet all the while, each of us is, in truth, a magnificent creator who exists in this world alone.

We Each Live Alone

A human being is born into this world alone. We also leave this world alone. And as we live in this world, we always live alone.

Though you may have a husband or a wife, a family, and friends, in the ultimate sense you must live your life on your own. You must live by your own will and your own power, for yours is a world of one. It is a world created and inhabited by you alone. Not even the spouse, partner, or children whom you love may enter that world, for it is a sacred place where you, and only you, determine your own health, your own thoughts, your own habits, and your own future.

Most of us think that we are living through the support, love, and care of our families, but this is an illusion. All human beings, by nature, must live alone in the worlds that they, themselves, are creating. Even if you are surrounded by a happy family, your worries, fears, anxieties, and sorrows are the product of your own thoughts, and can be resolved by you alone.

Of course, it is true that your loved ones and close friends will spare no effort in coming to your aid, but even so, the outcome depends on you alone. If you have taken a wrong turn, others can advise and warn you, but this is as far as it goes. They can tell you if they think you are being haughty or untruthful, or they can caution you to change your gloomy outlook, but unless you take their advice to heart, it will have no effect. In the end, it is you who choose whether to listen to it, accept it, act on it, or reject it.

From the outside, it may appear that others have determined your course in life, changed your fate, or healed your illness, but this can never happen. Everything about you is determined through your own authority, your own soul. That is the law of this world.

Why are people lucky or unlucky, healthy or frail, decisive or indecisive? Why do some become workaholics while others live only for amusement? What makes people conscientious, or respected, or well-liked, or unpopular? Why do some become leaders and others not? Each of us creates our own lifestyle and our own personality. How do we create it? Through our way of thinking.

Even if you are surrounded by wise and talented people who care for you and advise you, and even if you have achieved honor and fame through doing as they said, they did not determine your fate. Ultimately, it was you who listened to their advice and took it into your heart. The decision was yours, and so was the responsibility.

Each member of the human race has been given one individual life, radiating from the same universal source. Each life is precious, and each has its own sacred purpose. That is why each of us can think on our own, make decisions on our own, endure on our own, and act on our own. Each of us is responsible for doing what no one else can do, and each of us creates our destiny on our own. All human beings are inherently noble and absolutely equal.

This is why, even as an active member of a busy family, you nonetheless live completely on your own. If your heart holds feelings of loneliness, you can be lonely in the midst of a wonderful, loving family. On the other hand, even if you have no family at all, you can never be lonely if your thoughts are filled with people you love.

❧ Brighten Your Mind Through Your Own Efforts

The very same thing can be said about illness. Ultimately, the one who truly eases your illness is neither your doctor nor your family: it is you yourself. If you cannot believe in yourself and constantly experience uneasiness, worry, and fear, you are always planting seeds of illness and unhappiness in your heart. Though doctors, family members, and other capable people might do their best to encourage or even cure you, if your heart is unresponsive, or if you do not really believe what they say, there will be no effect at all.

If a team of doctors, friends, and relatives could stampede through your mind and try to root out the anxiety that you harbor there, do you think they could purge all traces of it? No one has the authority to do that, not even your closest friend or your most trusted physician. Not even God claims that right, for you are by nature the administrator of your own heart. It is a responsibility that you cannot escape from.

If you want to make your life shine, you must brighten your mind through your own efforts. Apart from you, there is no one in existence who can manage the workings of your own wondrous mind.

At this point in the Earth's history, humanity has not recognized this truth. We mistakenly think that others are responsible for giving us health and happiness. Since we do not realize that we create our own destiny with our own thought, we blindly believe that it is determined from the outside. This is why we think that the illness in our hearts can be cured by doctors, friends, or relatives. For the same reason, we believe that the cause of our depression or sorrow originates outside ourselves. This misconception is a fundamental problem for people today.

When illness, accidents, scandal, failure, fear, or other complications occur, they are your own responsibility. If your heart is filled with discontent, anger, or hatred, the cause stems from your own thinking. Never think that it was brought about by someone else. Even if your business has gone under, or you have been swindled, failed your exams, been disappointed in marriage, or betrayed by your children, never think that those conditions were created outside yourself. They were issues that involved you and no one else.

While most people can understand that we are all born alone, not everyone can agree that we also live alone. Very few people have become conscious of this. Once you have recognized this truth, if you engrave it deeply in your mind, you can free yourself from everything that troubles you, and you will see how simple and crystal-clear your life can be.

It might be extremely hard and painful for you to accept it, but I urge you to stand fast and face the truth with courage. Never try to run away from it. When you recognize that your illness, your inadequacy, and your unhappiness were of your own making, the course of your life will take a sharp turn for the better.

Do not leave your heart steeped in bitterness and discontent from one day to the next. It does no good at all to keep pouring in more sadness and apprehension. You must stop feeding the flames of hatred, jealousy, and anger. You are simply creating more problems for yourself.

Some might say: 'No, the cause is not in me. If my spouse had not been unfaithful, jealousy would never have sprung up in my heart,' or 'If I had not been swindled or betrayed, I would never have known resentment.' On the surface, these might seem like plausible arguments, but they are not the truth. All your anguish was born of your own thinking, and nothing more.

❧ Start Your Day with Luminous Thoughts

If you want to be happy, you must constantly plant seeds of happiness in your heart. Think to yourself: 'I'd like to be happy... I shall be happy... I must be happy.' Before you know it, you will naturally start thinking of ways to make yourself happy, and putting your ideas into practice.

Turn all your thoughts toward the positive. Fuel them with bright, constructive energy. Never allow dark, negative thoughts to occupy your mind. To accomplish this, it will be necessary for you to conduct a daily check of your thinking. If an even slightly negative thought crosses your mind, dispel it instantly with a world peace prayer, and switch your thoughts to positive ones.

Make this your routine practice, day after day. Give it a great deal of effort. At the moment you wake up in the morning, your very first thought sets the trend for your day. If you do not shake off yesterday's sluggishness and fatigue, or if you carry yesterday's mistakes, worries, and disappointments with you to the next morning, how can you expect to start your day feeling fresh and new? Unless you put a stop to them, the same negative feelings will crop up again and again.

A great many people start their days with a heavy, dismal, or irritated feeling. They dread starting work, and feel that their situation is bitter and painful. If you let thoughts like these stay with you, you will drag them with you for the entire day. Then, your day will turn out to be dreary, irksome, or excruciating, just as you expected.

If you wake up in the morning with the same sullen feeling that you had yesterday, it is up to you to dispel that feeling. You can do that by recognizing it as the aftermath of something you mistakenly thought or did in the past—a past that is meant to disappear. You can then let it be purified in a shining thought or a world peace prayer, and tell yourself that a new 'you' has been born as of today. Soon, you will start to behave exactly as you have said you would.

When you make up your mind that today will be a beautiful, refreshing day, your own actions will cause your belief to manifest itself and establish a new pattern in your life. This is why I urge you to always make a point of starting your day with wonderful thoughts, heavenly thoughts, thoughts that make you happy. Hold these thoughts in your mind. Force them to stay if you have to. Eventually, the conditions that you have repeatedly entertained in your mind will appear in this world.

Day after day, try to carry out small acts of good will, happiness, and gratitude. Before you know it, this will turn into a habit and you will naturally wake up each morning with happy feelings overflowing in your mind. Once you have reached this point, the rest is assured. From then on, your life will unfold in abundant joy, thankfulness and freedom. This is how you can create your own wonderful way of life.

Guides for the Future

In the twenty-first century, a great many people will begin living in this way. In doing so, they will serve as examples for humanity, so that we can all enhance our lives and create a brighter future.

Until recently, most of us have not known about the principles that govern this world. We have not realized that our own thoughts were responsible for creating our way of life. In the twenty-first century, humanity will seek the guidance of people who have firmly encountered this truth. Once we have chosen a bright path, old habits such as cheating ourselves, lying to ourselves, making excuses to ourselves, and blaming and judging ourselves will die out completely. Instead, we will naturally believe in loving and forgiving ourselves. We will aim only at pleasing our infinite, divine selves, and our lives will overflow with gratitude to the great universe.

A human being is born alone, lives alone, and dies alone. Once you recognize this, you will feel less and less need to lean on other people. Your being will grow stronger and stronger, until your whole existence demonstrates the divine truth of the universe.

With the arrival of the twenty-first century, it is my deep desire to foster the development of more and more people who live their wondrous lives to the very fullest.

You are the Universe.

First published in January 1995

CHAPTER 4

Guide Yourself to Happiness

From the outset, a human being should radiate light. This is because we are by nature light itself. Our light cannot be sought or discovered outside ourselves. We must *be* that light. All of humanity must return to its original light and become one with it.

Since you are your own light, you must become the true guide of your own destiny. Your destiny must never be guided by anyone other than yourself, or by anything that exists separately from you. If you always rely on external guidance, without getting in touch with the light that is the most intrinsic part of you, you will not truly be able to direct the course of your noble and precious life.

This lifetime of yours is meant to be lived by you alone. The life-energy to live it is yours and no one else's. If you overlook this crucial point and think of your life as something controlled by an outside force, what do you suppose your existence really consists of? If you are not the life of the universe itself, then what on earth are you, and to what end are you meant to make use of the wisdom, individuality, freedom, and creative abilities that you were born with?

The wondrous, infinite wisdom that shines within you was not given to you so that you could submit yourself to the will of others. Your divine wisdom was apportioned to you so that it could be manifested through your existence. The more you make use of it, the more you will polish and enhance it. As you keep living this way, you will ultimately raise yourself to the point where your own wisdom flows and interchanges with the essential wisdom of the universe. At that time, it will become possible for you to freely manifest the divine functions of the universe without any interference.

Most of us, however, prefer an easier approach to life, and so we content ourselves with lackadaisically relying on an external force or else placing our destiny in the hands of other people. Instead of activating the divine wisdom that radiates infinitely within us, we have buried it in a far corner of our minds. Then, we seek wisdom from outside us, by appealing to an external God to rescue us from our miseries.

Most of us do not believe in our own inherent wisdom. We undervalue our abilities, doubt our own brilliance, and take no notice of the infinite healing power that resides within us. Virtually all of humanity has lost sight of its original, divine image. We thoroughly believe ourselves to be weak, short-lived, useless beings who have nothing in common with God. Turning a blind eye to the health and intelligence that abound within us, we focus our attention on our negative habits and our feelings of inferiority. Given this state of mind, even if we occasionally make a sudden, desperate attempt at drawing out our inner splendor, our efforts often miss the mark and end up being wasted.

This occurs because most of us have detached ourselves from our intrinsic truth. Being oblivious to our original identity, we have taken to bemoaning our misfortunes, sighing over our troubles, and tormenting ourselves over our illnesses. Though we strive, endure, and deny ourselves, we are misusing our energy, and since we are pouring all our strength into a fierce battle against life, our efforts never bring us peace and happiness. Our only rewards are more misery, suffering, trouble, and illness.

To reverse this situation, I feel that we need a completely new approach to life. We need to realign our consciousness and our way of living with our inner truth.

❧ Identify the Nature of Your Problems

Up to now, we human beings have been constantly seeking to resolve our suffering and misery by appealing for outside help from God, and in doing so we have, indeed, arrived at some solutions. Yet, since we have not made any fundamental change in our own mentality, which first gave rise to those problems, the same problems cannot help but re-emerge later on. And each time this happens, we again hope to be rescued from the outside.

Until each of us resolves for ourselves the question of why the same difficulties and worries keep arising, we will never be able to shake ourselves free from them. We will only keep circling round and round in the same rut, thinking, 'Why does this keep happening to me? Why is each day so oppressive and hard to bear? Why do others resent me? Why can't I live in peace among my own family and acquaintances?'

And so the cycle continues. Difficult problems keep piling up and taking shape in our lives. And until we resolve the fundamental question of why this happens, we will not attain lasting peace and happiness. The key to knowing why, I feel, is to closely observe and know ourselves. If we know nothing at all about who we truly are, even though we may agitate ourselves by telling ourselves that we are unhappy, ill, or beset with disasters, it will not lead to a solution. The first and most important thing we can do is to know ourselves well, and to identify the nature of the worries and misfortunes that keep following us about.

How do you go about this? You can begin with the simplest of things. First, clearly ask yourself whether you are now happy or unhappy. Should the answer be that you are unhappy, your next step is to identify the nature of your unhappy feelings. Be honest with yourself and closely examine these feelings, directly and straightforwardly, to see what they really consist of. What is it that is binding your heart? What thought is it that gives you pain and inhibits your freedom? What thought is at the root of the unhappiness and fear that have sunk into your mind?

In truth, happiness comes naturally to every human being. Living in happiness is our natural state of being. Yet a great many of us have imposed on ourselves a way of life that is just the opposite of happiness. We suffer without end, never discerning what is going on in our own hearts and minds. When advised to honestly examine our thoughts, we find that they are so complex and bizarre that we hardly know where to begin.

Even though our innermost thoughts are our own private domain, we are nonetheless afraid to observe them. We feel that we need to summon enormous courage simply to take stock of our own emotions. Most of us would rather not know about them. We would rather let the matter remain unclear.

Our impulse is to cover up all our stored thoughts and feelings with a huge veil, and stow them away somewhere.

This kind of reluctance is understandable. However, if we really want to steer our destiny in a brighter direction, sooner or later a time will come when we will have to closely observe what is going on in our own minds.

Most of us are aware that we do not want our own frailties to be observed by others, but this is not our foremost problem. The main thing that closes the door on our future is our unwillingness to lay our hearts bare to ourselves. It is our inclination to hide our innermost feelings from ourselves, leaving them undisclosed, untouched, and unaltered. But we do not recognize this.

If you are in this situation, it is time to let everything inside you come naturally out into the light. There is no need to be afraid of anything, nor is there anything that you need to feel ashamed of. You are not alone in your weakness—it is shared by all human beings. Take courage, and face up to your secrets. Face up to the events of your past. You need not fear them, run from them, or conceal them any longer. Take courage and recognize them. Recognize the wounds and the deceptions of the past. Recognize the pain, the embarrassment, and the dismal feelings. They must not remain repressed forever. Let them rise to the surface of your mind, then let them go. Let them vanish forever, as they are meant to do. Take courage, and free yourself from them at the earliest possible moment.

You can free yourself from the secrets that are the source of your pain. You can let them be extinguished in the light that you are emitting when you wish and pray for the peace of humanity. If your painful secrets are to vanish completely, you must continue to send out light and surround yourself with light.

❧ God Does Not Help Us Escape

On the other hand, if you persist in keeping old thoughts and feelings buried within you while at the same time trying to run away from them, you will never be free from them, and all your solutions will be temporary ones.

This is similar to what happens when you try to forget the gloom in your mind for a while by borrowing the strength of alcohol. Once the influence of the alcohol has waned, the old aching starts to surface again. The alcohol did not solve the problem. Its relief was only a form of make-believe. Later on, the same sense of uneasiness and oppression assails you once again.

A human being's destiny does not come into full bloom until one faces up to one's own pain and allows it to vanish. Until then, there can be no true spiritual peace and awakening. When we continually refuse to face up to ourselves, we are actually sentencing ourselves to a life of superficiality and camouflage, and we become magnets for misfortune, illness, trouble, and despair.

Once we have chosen this kind of life, many of us get into the habit of begging and pleading with God to neutralize our suffering and grant us a moment of serenity. If, indeed, this practice could promise us ultimate freedom of mind, our joy would be unparalleled. Yet, throughout the world, I do not think there has ever been anyone whose mind has attained lasting freedom and happiness by begging God for help. This is because begging God for outside help is different from true prayer. It is an aberration of prayer. Our innermost selves should know this best of all. However, when one has lost touch with truth, this point becomes difficult to grasp.

Thus, a great many of us feel spiritually unfulfilled, and we swing this way and that in search of equilibrium. As we wander, our hearts hunger and thirst for refreshment. It is as if your throat were parched, and you tried to satisfy your longing for water with something else. Though you have always known that the only thing that can quench your thirst is water, you think that water cannot be obtained. So, you deceive yourself into thinking that it is not water that you need, but something else. You then search for something else, as a substitute for water. In reality, though, only water can quench your thirst. No matter how many substitutes for water you try, you do not feel satisfied. Though you have forced yourself to endure the absence of water, though you have spurred yourself on and tried to make do with something other than water, striving to convince yourself that you can be satisfied that way, though you may feign contentment, your thirst continues, just as before.

❧ Accurately Read the Messages from Your True Mind

Isn't this the primary way in which you are deceiving yourself? A voice within you keeps crying out, telling you what your true self is seeking, what your true self wants to do, and how your true self wants to live joyfully, but this inner cry is being smothered and held back. You are the one who holds it back. You are ignoring the cry of your own true mind.

Perhaps you have a particular aim in mind, something that you would enjoy doing. It would be easy enough to do if you simply set about doing it. But the trouble is, you are stifling the voice of your own mind. You say to yourself: 'What would my parents think? What would people say? They might laugh at me! I haven't got the courage for it anyway, and I don't think I have the ability either. I don't have enough confidence to do what would make me happy. I might end up being totally frustrated.'

Concern over what others might think or say is one of the biggest obstacles that confront us when we think about walking forward along the path that would bring us joy. As a result, uneasiness pervades our mind, and we think: 'Will it be all right? Perhaps I'd better quit. Yes, I'll take the accepted way, the way that offers security.' Thus, we turn from the path that our heart truly wants to follow and opt for the path that others are following.

Yet in doing so, we find that our inner discord continues. Dissatisfaction, resentment, and hurriedness never seem to fade from our mind. We feel no sense of accomplishment, and never seem able to find a task into which we can put all our energy. We see no other choice for ourselves than to go on living in discontent as our energy keeps smoldering and spluttering for no apparent reason.

If we caught a glimpse of our own past thoughts, we might recall the timidity and lack of conviction that we felt at a time when we made certain decisions about the course that our life would take. Perhaps we have some sense of regret or guilt over the effects that our decisions are having now. Yet we conclude that after having lived this way for so long, it would not make sense for us to change direction at this point in our life. On top of that, we might feel reluctant to give up the various gains that we have accumulated through our years of effort, hardship, suffering, and endurance. We would rather not admit to ourselves, in all humility, that we failed to guide ourselves in the direction that we really wanted to go. Because of this, we continue to cheat and deceive ourselves, and force ourselves to persevere along the same path as before.

Deep down, however, we do not feel satisfied. Our inner self wants to reject the old way of life and undertake a totally new one. Yet we feel bound to keep suppressing those feelings. Thus, we put pressure on ourselves and try to persuade ourselves to continue walking along a path that we dislike, and that awakens no joy in us.

In this way, a great many of us are in pain because our way of life betrays the urging of our inner self. We feel restricted by our lack of ability to change ourselves now, at this late date. Despite our continued tedium, weariness, and suffering, we just carry on as we did before.

Though living each day with joy and purpose is the very path that leads people to spiritual peace and awakening, virtually no one is living that way. To a greater or lesser degree, all of us are deceiving our true selves and creating frustration in our own mind. It is like wanting water but not receiving it. It is like drinking a substitute for water and trying to persuade yourself that you are content that way. Yet how could anyone be content with a substitute for water? Even if your thirst were temporarily relieved, you would soon feel thirsty again.

Prior to being deceived by others, we always deceive ourselves. If we continue to deceive and betray ourselves, even though we may ask God to remove our pain, sadness, and anxiety, no lasting solution can come about.

Activate All Your Energy

Even now, it is not too late to make a new start. First, look deep within yourself, asking, 'Am I happy or not? Do I live each day with a joyful feeling, or not?' The answers to these questions must be clearly established. Even if you succeed in finding short-term solutions to the troubles that surface in your life, if you do not face these fundamental questions, sooner or later you will again be confronted by similar problems.

The only way that we human beings can use all of the energy given to us is by faithfully following the urging of our own hearts. This is because each of us commands the will and the power to carry our own heart's desire through to its completion. This will and this power are naturally called forth and activated at the time when we joyfully pour all our effort, concentration, and life-energy into doing what we really want to do, sustained by a sense of meaningfulness and inner happiness. This ability and power that we possess to carry out our will cannot be set in motion by a mind that deceives itself. Instead of being fully ignited, our original energy and power end up smoldering in a state of incomplete combustion, because they are being used in a distorted way.

To put your true abilities into action, it is necessary in everything you do to correctly read the messages that are coming from your true mind. Even if your idea seems preposterous and unattainable, if it is something you desire with your whole being, from a spirit of joy and happiness, and if you feel that it is truly worthwhile, you will definitely be able to turn your dream into reality. This is because your genuine, heartfelt desire activates the full breadth of your strength, your energy, and your innate human ability to carry any thought to fruition.

Suppose that you wish to achieve something very small, a trifling thing that no one else cares about or takes the trouble to reach for. If you really want it from the bottom of your heart, then, as you work your way toward your goal, that trifling thing will connect with something bigger, and your wish will be fulfilled within a larger setting, bringing wondrous results that serve to further expand and develop your life.

Why is it, I wonder, that most of us cannot be honest with ourselves about our own lives? Those who are honest with themselves can live in peace and supreme bliss. Conversely, no one deceives oneself more than a person who experiences a great deal of anxiety, suffering, and misery. There is nothing sadder than to ignore the wishes of one's own heart for the sake of appearances, vanity, or lack of confidence. Those of us who live that way have not noticed that we eventually receive a 'bill' for each and every time we have deceived or lied to ourselves. This is the way most human beings are living right now.

❧ One at a Time, Neatly and Cleanly...

It is quite natural for us to become ill if we do not experience joy in our daily life. Those who find life worthwhile and live each day with joy and vitality never make themselves ill at all. This is because life, in its natural state, shines brightly. When we feel frustrated, however, our thoughts are not cheerful or shining. Instead, we always feel hurried or fretful, and our uneasy thoughts generate worry and unpleasantness. These feelings then determine the course of our daily lives.

How can cheerful, happy days be born from such thinking? How can a happy life come to be? Such thinking can only produce illness, mishap, disaster, and suffering.

But it is not too late. Everyone has the power to guide their own precious life straight into a world of joy and happiness. Won't you please guide yourself so that joy constantly wells up from your mind, making you cheerful and happy? This is what each of us truly longs for. Once we can faithfully follow the messages that spring from our true mind, we will never meet with misfortune, illness, or accidents.

What each of us must do for ourselves now is to closely and carefully study our own mind. This is by no means difficult, and there is nothing at all to be afraid of. All we have to do is to look squarely at the actual conditions that have presented themselves. All we have to do is to clearly perceive and acknowledge whether we have betrayed our true selves. We must steadfastly observe our own thoughts, while at the same time firmly linking ourselves with the infinite wisdom, love, and power of the universe.

As we begin this process, a great many disagreeable or uncomfortable feelings may manifest themselves. This is because all the worrisome or painful thoughts that we have created have to reveal themselves eventually, in order to vanish from our hearts. And once they have faded and vanished, there will be no need to call them back again.

Our self-deceit, too, is destined to fade away. The same can be said about our lack of resolve, which first caused us to follow a road we did not want to follow, a road of other people's choosing. We must remember that nothing in this world happens randomly or by accident. Everything occurs by necessity in this world, in the process of fading away. As each condition emerges and vanishes, our lives will surely become happier.

It is important for us to steadily believe this and to practice it day by day. Just understanding it theoretically is of no use at all. We have to put it into practice, thoroughly and properly, each time something untrue or unharmonious emerges in our thoughts or in our lives. One way to do this is to greet each unwelcome feeling or circumstance with the thought, 'Fading

away—May peace prevail on Earth.' Another way is to counter it with a bright thought like 'Infinite betterment!' or 'Infinite
light!'[9]

Without begrudging ourselves the effort that it takes, without groaning, sighing, or feeling disgusted, we must identify
our emotionally charged thoughts one at a time, neatly and
cleanly. We must recognize them, understand them, and let
them vanish. One by one, we must let each turbulent thought
or feeling be utterly eliminated from our hearts as we steadily
attune ourselves to our inner light. As those old, unharmonious thoughts and feelings keep dissipating one by one, our
true, shining selves will gradually appear.

Make a Pledge to be Happy

Once your true self has begun to surface, you will find that you
are being reborn to your true way of life. You will be able to
guide yourself closer and closer to your true, infinite self.

To guide yourself forward, you must carefully tune in to
the messages coming from your true self, for you are the only
one who can receive them. There is no one who can receive
them for you. There is no one who can give you what your
heart is calling for. Even if a reasonable, generally-accepted
answer is provided to you, it only reflects the median condition. It does not come from you. The purpose of your life is to
catch the messages coming from your own true mind, so that
you can walk your own path with joy.

What can you do if you do not know how to attune yourself to the messages coming from your true self? One thing you
can do is to pray continuously for the peace of humanity. From
within your prayer, the resonance of your true self will be felt,

and its voice will clearly and accurately guide you to happiness. This is what you are here for. This is why you were born in this world.

In the past, you may have thought that you were living your life, but it was not truly yours. You did as you were told, or you behaved a certain way because you cared so much about appearances, or about your reputation, or about your family's traditions. Or, perhaps it was because you did not believe in yourself. Though the reasons may differ, the result is the same—your way of life did not spring from your own true self.

From now on, for the remainder of this lifetime, if you do your very best to be true to the real *you*, you will surely overcome your suffering, and in the end you will be able to leave this world in radiance.

Suffering, distress, anxiety, fear—all these have taken shape because of the times when your way of life ran counter to the true *you*. Once you have recognized this, there will be no need at all for you to repeat the same senseless mistakes again and again.

Never forget to fill every corner of your mind with the will to be happy. Each morning when you wake up, make a pledge to yourself that today, all day, you will steadily guide yourself toward happiness. From the moment when you make this pledge, the power of your mind will align itself with your command, and start working hard to fill your day with happiness. Then, at the end of the day, just before you retire for the night, here is what I would suggest: If it has been a happy day, so much the better. If not, do your best to persuade yourself that tomorrow, you will make a fresh start and steer yourself toward happiness. By encouraging yourself in this way every day, you will naturally start to adjust yourself to the will of the true *you*, and a radiant way of life will spread out before you.

❧ Knowing Yourself is Knowing the Universe

Whatever you do, please do not fall back into the foolishness of shutting out and losing touch with what is most precious and wonderful in you. This is why each of us needs to continuously scrutinize our own mind and come to know our own true self. In knowing our true selves, we will know the universe. If we do not know our true selves, it will not be possible for us to know the universe.

Knowing the universe is the same as knowing love. Once we are able to truly know the love that dwells within us, we will simultaneously know all love, and this means that we will know the love of the universe.

It is the same with a drop of seawater. If you have succeeded in knowing all there is to know about a drop of seawater, you will know everything about the sea, since the entire sea is present in that one single drop. That's why, if you wish to know what the sea is, there is no need to travel to all the continents to survey all the seas. There is no need to gather knowledge from all directions, bringing in all the various sciences, and conducting experiments on the seas. All you need to do is closely observe that one drop and come to know it thoroughly—then you will know the entirety of the sea. By examining that one drop, you will understand that the sea is salty. If the composition of that one drop of seawater is H_2O and $NaCl$, you will know that the entire sea is composed of hydrogen, oxygen, sodium and chlorine. If you have discovered the essence of a drop of seawater, you have discovered the essence of the sea.

The same is true for the universe. If you wish to know the nature of the universe, it is not necessary to travel to all the galaxies to inspect all the stars. All you need to do is observe the one universal ray that resonates within you. When you have succeeded in knowing your true self, you will also know the universe. You will comprehend the truth of all human beings.

If you begin to project this ultimate truth into your own heart, and let its image be depicted there, you will discover a new self that is completely unlike your former self. You will see a radiant being who is one with the entire universe. And when others see you, they too will be able to feel the love of the universe. Until we reach that state, it is very, very important for us to steadily practice returning to oneness with our true, infinite selves.

You are the Universe.

First published in July 1995

CHAPTER 5

True
Forgiveness

All our pain and suffering come from one source. They come from not knowing the truth. Only when we know the truth can we begin to forgive ourselves for our past errors.

We have been torturing ourselves. We have been treating ourselves like miserable, sinful, greedy creatures who have to beg for divine forgiveness, but this is not who we really are. Our sins and errors are not forgiven by a an external being called 'God.' They are forgiven by the God that exists within us.

In the past, we believed that we had to beg and plead with God to forgive us from the outside. We thought that sins were forgiven in this way, but it cannot be so. It is the inner God who must forgive us. If we do not forgive ourselves for our own wrongs, we will never be free from them.

We are not being guided from a faraway corner of heaven. We are being guided from within, by our inner divinity. This is why, until we have forgiven ourselves for our mistakes, our feelings of guilt will never go away. If we do not know this truth, we cannot expect our suffering to be healed.

We human beings, who have divinity within us, are the life

of the universe itself. We must know this essential truth with our whole being, and never lose sight of it. We must know that infinite love, infinite forgiveness, and infinite gratitude are steadily resonating within us at all times, constantly sending forth intensely brilliant light.

No matter how much conventional knowledge we may have acquired, and no matter how well versed we may be in world affairs, if our awareness stops there, it means that we are totally uninformed about truth. This is because this kind of knowledge tells us nothing at all about what human beings most need to know. Not only that, the superficial knowledge that we have accumulated is driving us farther and farther from the truth.

Our essential consciousness is the principle of creation— the spirit of the universe itself. Our original being is perfect and integral. At the source of our life, there is no such thing as illness or discord. If things like this occur temporarily, it is caused by the human consciousness losing touch with its source.

While we work as creators in this world, we might pray to the great God of the universal law, pleading for our unhappy conditions to be set right. Yet the universal law does not perform that function directly. This is because there is no such thing as illness, poverty, suffering, or misery at the level of the universal law. Likewise, the mechanism for healing those ills is not found at that level either. It occurs within us. Forgiveness, too, occurs within us.

Certainly, there are people whose sufferings were fully healed when they prayed, entreated, and clung to God, but that alone does not explain it. As they prayed, those people awakened to their inner, divine love, and this enabled them to forgive themselves. It was not that the universal law forgave them directly.

The great universal law guides everything according to the cosmic principle of harmony. This is all it does. It does not perform the function of responding to each person's wishes directly. It only governs the movement of the universe, maintaining large-scale harmony.

The love of the universe works through our guardian spirits and divinities to guide and protect us. These protective beings are always working within us and around us, to let us see the truth and awaken to it. Day and night, they are supporting us with their complete and unconditional love, and urging us to call forth our own divinity. Yet even they cannot forgive our errors. This power is held only by our inner, divine self.

❧ Advancing Toward Our True Selves

The unhappiness, illness, suffering, and wrongdoing that we have generated can be reconciled by ourselves alone. Why, then, did the great saints of the past not tell us this? If those holy ones had directly conveyed such a great truth to the people of their day, there would have been no one to understand it, because people's understanding had not yet evolved that far.

And so, in past times, great saints taught people to entrust all their sins to God, and that if they did this, God would ease all their miseries. This teaching was not, in itself, an ultimate goal. It was a means for turning our attention toward the divine. It was one step in a process for shifting our consciousness to a point where we could recognize ourselves as divine beings.

If, right from the start, those saints had bluntly announced that human beings have divinity within them, they would not have guided even one person to an awakening. In view of this, they introduced a method that religious people could follow: pray to God and depend on God.

People with an intellectual turn of mind, however, do not like to ask God to forgive their offenses. They deeply feel that they themselves must compensate for their own wrongs. It never occurs to them that the wrongs they have committed can be forgiven through entreaty and supplication, which they consider to be signs of weakness. This is one major reason why intellectuals often turn toward materialism. Unfortunately however, materialistic theory bears no resemblance to universal divine truth.

Most of humanity does not yet know the reality of its existence, which is why our suffering is so intense. Since we do not discern the divinity that exists within us, we continue to plead with an external God for forgiveness. Until we profoundly believe that our wrongs have been forgiven, our suffering cannot be eased. And this will happen only when we truly believe in our own forgiveness.

Those past teachings which instructed people to entreat God for forgiveness were very helpful and necessary. Without those teachings, virtually no one would have been able to rise above his or her suffering. Such were the conditions thousands of years ago, but not today.

Also, in olden times, people lived in societies without the modern conveniences that we take for granted. In this more materialistic age, people's suffering has consequently taken an entirely different form.

Take illness, for example. In the past, illnesses seem to have been less diverse than they are today. For the most part, people used to contract simple, contagious diseases. Today's illnesses, as well as the methods of diagnosis, are entirely different. They are far more complex, and straightforward treatment often seems impossible.

Emotional strife, too, has taken on a different character. The nature and intensity of people's mental anguish has changed, and it brings different consequences. Simple things are becoming complicated, and overlapping causes are becoming more and more entangled.

How do we explain these changes? With the natural movement of the universe, everything is advancing toward higher dimensions. The speed of everything is increasing. When humanity does not follow this natural movement by attuning itself to the laws of peace and harmony, its discord increases and its suffering grows more and more acute.

Humanity is continually evolving, every second of every day. From one instant to the next, we are drawing closer and closer to our original, universal selves. Today, there are people who are beginning to call forth their own divinity. In past times, there were few we know of who did this—Jesus, Sakyamuni Buddha, and a few others. Nowadays, though, there are people in many countries who come close to the mental state of those saints.

Since these people have already started awakening to their inner truth, they no longer seek forgiveness or healing from a force outside themselves. Though they pray earnestly, they are praying only for the harmony of the universe to reveal itself through the vessels of their physical bodies. They are praying only for peace to prevail on Earth.

Such people already know what true prayer is. Their

prayers are exalted and pure. Truth is starting to reflect itself in their words and behavior. They know the means of attaining forgiveness for their past mistakes. Even if they have committed colossal errors, they do not expect their burden to be removed from the outside. They know that this cannot be done. Their prayers are neither pleas nor requests. Rather, they are prayers for a deeper awakening and a greater manifestation of truth.

Why is Humanity Still Suffering?

A great many people have thought that if they prayed to an external God, asking to be forgiven for their corruption and errors, all of it would be resolved from the outside by the great, merciful divine love. Indeed, a large number of people have deeply believed that an external God's radiant light would heal their physical bodies and give them everything they wished for.

Yet if an external God has forgiven us for everything, why is humanity still suffering? If an external God had forgiven all our sins, there would be no reason for our pain to continue. Somehow, things are not exactly as they seemed.

After we prayed to a faraway God, did our heavy sense of guilt entirely vanish? Do our hearts now soar in perfect freedom? Do our souls sparkle with hope? If so, all of us must be new, radiant people, free from the gloominess that we felt before.

Why, then, do people's expressions still hold such sadness? Why do our hearts sink into such dark depression? Are we still laden with a heavy burden? If so, what is the reason for it? Did we not beg and plead with God? Since we so earnestly besought God to lift our burdens, heal our illnesses, and dissolve our miseries, why do they still remain? Does it mean that God did not hear our prayers, or will not answer our requests?

If God answered our prayers in this way, human suffering would have ended long ago. If an external God granted us all our desires, we should each be overwhelmed with bliss. If an external God could banish all our afflictions, we should already have been relieved of our illnesses. Wars should have ceased to exist. Each of us should be singing life's praises, free from all care. But such is not the case. Why has God kept silent?

Deep within, each of us knows the answer: regardless of our pleas, regardless of our prayers, the great universal God only continues to maintain the laws of harmony, governing the movement of the universe, and watching over the evolution of humanity. Omniscient and omnipotent, the infinite God never intervenes. It only gives. It only continues to provide us with an endless supply of love, light, and energy.

When people pray to the Almighty for their sins to be forgiven, how could it be that some are forgiven and others not? Would this not be unjust? Would God not forgive all people without favoritism? What would qualify a person for God's forgiveness? What recourse would there be for the unforgiven ones? If, despite their prayers, human beings were deserted by God in their weakness, whatever would be their purpose in this world?

It is time for each and every person to come face to face with the truth: it is not possible that some are forgiven by God while others are not. The universal God, or universal law, as such, does not directly function through the dimension where sins are forgiven or not forgiven. If the universal law were to forgive our sins, it would surely forgive the sins of all humanity. But the universal law never does this.

❧ Forgiveness Comes from Within

What, then, is the difference between people whose sins are forgiven after praying to God and those whose sins remain unforgiven? To all appearances, it may seem that the sins of the former were forgiven through their prayers to an external God. In reality, though, it is because those people were able to forgive themselves. People whose sins remain unforgiven even after praying are those who cannot forgive themselves in their hearts.

Why does this difference occur? It comes from the wide gap between those who are conscious of divine truth and those who are not. People who have awakened to the truth know that they are always abundantly receiving new life and energy from the divine source of their being. They know how to give expression to their perfect, original selves while living in this world.

Once we have comprehended the essential principle that humans are infinite beings, everything else becomes clear to us. We come to recognize that any difficulty, any misery, any affliction is sure to vanish as soon as it appears. Knowing this, we never grasp at any kind of agony, or fix our attention on it. We simply let it pass by.

Here is our key to success: do not hold on to any misfortune, hindrance, discord, or calamity. Do not to attach yourself to it. Do not fear it or worry about it. Do not shrink from it or try to escape from it. This is our passport to spiritual freedom. We must use it well.

Once we become clearly conscious of our true human identity as rays of infinite divine light, we know that darkness is no match for light. An infinite being cannot be imperfect or afflicted with discord. Because we are all children of God, we are all capable of manifesting our perfect, divine image.

If we are to live fully, as we were meant to live, we must know well who we truly are. We must realize that our inner self is innocent of all corruption and hatred, and is at all times whole and complete. We must know that our true self is innately provided with an abundance of everything that we need.

Unlimited love, unlimited prosperity, unlimited harmony, unlimited goodness: all these limitless qualities are inherent in a human being. Sin, corruption, hatred, anger, sorrow, and pain do not fundamentally exist. Yet, we grasp at things that have no reality, saying that they are there. We accuse ourselves and accuse others, judge ourselves and judge others. This is how we demean and torment ourselves. Meanwhile, finding the pain unendurable, we try to lean on an external image of God and entreat it for forgiveness. This cycle has been perpetuated since human beings first lost sight of the truth.

Throughout history, humanity has been turning round and round in circles. We have been tying ourselves in knots, depriving ourselves of our freedom, tormenting ourselves, and driving ourselves down into misery. In the end, we have made ourselves ill, and have thrust ourselves into darkness. Meanwhile, though all these problems derive from our own emotions, thoughts, and behavior, we have been expecting an external being to save us from them all.

How can the universal God remove pain that it did not inflict? If painful feelings had originally been sent from God, it would be perfectly natural to expect God to take them away.

But since we human beings willfully created our own ills, it makes no sense at all to seek a cure from the outside. The solution must lie within us. Our sins will be removed only when we have forgiven ourselves.

Converting Our Thoughts to Light

For those of you who find it hard to forgive yourselves, here is a suggestion: do good things, one after another. As you keep on doing more and more good things with a strong and positive will, your guilty feelings will naturally diminish. They will seem less and less important to you. Instead of struggling with them day after day, your heart trembling with fear and shame, try pouring all your energy into strengthening your will to do good things.

As you continue to think this way, you will naturally begin to do good things. Your joyful actions will fill your mind with thoughts of gratitude and fulfillment. No longer obsessed with guilt, your heart will become free and bright. You will stop holding on to the past, and your inner self will start to surface in your daily life. Confidence and courage will surge forth, guiding you toward a joyous way of living.

In urging yourself to undertake positive actions, you might envision a variety of things you can do: being kind to others, loving others, helping others, guiding or rescuing others. All these are, of course, good things. Yet there is something more you can do. Fill your thoughts with light at every moment. Draw forth all that is infinite within you: infinite love, infinite gratitude, infinite light, infinite prosperity, infinite happiness, infinite potential. Let these infinite qualities find expression in your conscious thoughts.

Always ward off negative words and actions. Try never to use words such as 'dirty,' 'bad,' 'sick,' 'ugly,' 'angry,' 'can't,' 'hate,' or 'impossible.' Try never to express jealousy, complaint, or resentment in your emotions. If you do your best to consciously reject thoughts like these, you have accomplished something marvelous.

It may be easy to understand this in theory, but when it comes to actually doing it, we tend to unconsciously express negative words and emotions quite easily. With practice, though, you can make it part of your natural behavior to positively send out only bright thoughts, words and actions. When you reach this point, you will be able to forgive yourself for the very first time.

If you cannot forgive yourself now, decisively fling yourself into a stream of bright thinking. Immerse your soul in brightness. Think luminous thoughts and perform shining actions. This is your road to true forgiveness.

Love Your True Self

Ultimately, you must be able to forgive yourself for your own errors. Even if you do not know this, as long as you believe in the absolute, infinite energy and power of universal, divine love, and fully entrust yourself to it, your trust will open your heart to truth. Without consciously recognizing it, you will have, indeed, forgiven yourself.

On the other hand, if your suffering is not eased after praying for forgiveness, it means that you doubt yourself and do not trust in divine love. You might be rigidly convinced that God would never be kind enough to forgive such a sinful person as you. Because you harbor doubts as to the immense love and power of the divine, you cannot call forth the power to guide yourself. When you harbor even the slightest doubt, you cannot let go of your past errors.

If you truly wish to be happy, you must love yourself with all your heart. If you do not love yourself, and keep hating and cursing yourself, how can you possibly expect to be happy? How can you forgive yourself if you mistrust yourself, doubt your own ability, and neglect your own life? It is time to wake up, as soon as possible. You must know who you really are.

You may have committed a sin so grave that you can tell it to no one. You may have hated yourself beyond forgiveness. Yet you must know that your sin was not created by the real *you*. All your misdeeds were manifestations of your mistaken thoughts—images formed by your illusions. They took shape in your fate so that they could disappear from your subconscious, where they had been hiding. The shapes and forms of things always vanish as soon as they appear. Tell yourself that, as your mistakes vanish, everything will become better from this moment on.

Your true self radiates divine light. Your true self is life-energy, radiating from the source of the universe. The infiniteness of the universe is enshrined in you. Sin is an impermanent event. Anger, hatred, strife, jealousy, and resentment are short-lived phenomena. They occur in order to erase themselves from your subconscious. They are not inherent to you. How pointless it is to give your heart over to those impermanent conditions, constricting your freedom and spoiling your happiness. You do this because your thoughts have fixed themselves in the past. You have been shutting out the truth.

You can forgive yourself for all the events of the past. You need not accuse yourself so unremittingly, for as long as you keep clinging to your shame, it will not go away. To whatever extent you cannot forgive yourself, you will have to keep on carrying that same amount of pain with you. Your pain will continue until you have forgiven yourself.

Originally, the human spirit is empowered to forgive any kind of offense. The evils that were stirred up through our ignorance can be dispelled through our divine wisdom. When we know this, we have opened our eyes to truth. Our suffering will have vanished, because we have recognized that it had no true and lasting substance.

At this late date, we cannot spare the time for regretting each of our mistakes from the past. Instead, let us fill our minds with infinite light and energy. Let us steadily convert all our thoughts to powerfully bright ones, from moment to moment, hour to hour, and day to day. Before we are aware of it, our guilt will have healed.

Living in this way, we are enlivened with a bright, enthusiastic feeling. Our thoughts are free from worry, fear, and blame. We have fully melted into the love of the universe.

As people around the world continue to pray for peace on Earth, more and more of us are awakening and striving to bring about wonderful changes in society. As we proceed through the twenty-first century, a great transformation is about to take place in the hearts of humanity. It will be achieved through each and every one of us.

You are the Universe.

First published in October 1994

CHAPTER 6

Praise Your Mind

To be honest, I look forward to the time when human beings will have outgrown the need for organized religions.

When I see how very many people continue to be deceived, swindled, threatened, or frightened by a religion, I feel that I can hardly endure it. Those who are cheating others are, of course, in the wrong, but in my view, the ones being cheated are also in error, because both sides are equally unaware of the truth.

More often than not, people join a religion when they are feeling weak and confused, or burdened with a great deal of suffering and misery. That is why they look to a religion for relief. Essentially, religion is a means of explaining the absolute truth and universal law. In addition, it has the role of teaching and guiding people with regard to life and death. Nowadays, though, many religions have wholly deviated from their original path. Is it because a bewildered populace has strayed from the right track, or could it be that the clergy and religious administrators have lost their footing? I feel that it is probably a combination of both.

When we take a good look at contemporary religions, we

find a great many organizations that seem unworthy of the title 'religion.' Indeed, they owe their existence to the fact that so many people are ready to put their trust in them. The reason why such religions have become so popular is that so many people are unhappy, distressed, ailing, suffering, and lacking in strength, and do not understand who they really are. There are far too many of us who have no idea at all of the value of our existence, the meaning of our lives, or the importance of our daily words, thoughts, and actions. Since we do not know what we are living for, we have forgotten how to believe in ourselves.

As there are so many people in this condition, I would like to offer a few simple guidelines aimed at helping people tell the difference between true religions and false ones.

A true religion explains and clarifies truth, law, and the Way. A true religion does not aim specifically at worldly benefits, or at fostering a thriving business, or at the healing of physical illnesses. Of course, during the process of drawing out our inner truth, it is not unusual for our misfortune, disharmony, disease, and suffering to be eased in a natural way. This is because while we are progressing toward our ultimate path, we raise ourselves up and become brighter, our mistaken ideas fade away, and all sorts of favorable conditions and material benefits spontaneously appear. Therefore, sickness is healed, suffering fades away, and our lives become more harmonious.

Yet even though one may have attained such benefits through a true religion, this is not its final objective. The goal of any true religion is for each and every person to raise themselves up until they reach oneness with their divine self, meaning that they manifest infinite love, infinite wisdom, infinite health, and infinite life itself through their physical existence. A religion that guides people toward this goal can indeed be called a true religion.

On the other hand, counterfeit religions tend to involve one or more of the following practices:

(1) Extolling worldly benefits on a large scale by saying, for example, that if you join that faith, your sickness will be cured, or that you will acquire psychic or spiritual powers, or that your business will thrive, and so on.

(2) Preying on people's weaknesses and extracting large sums of money from them, using words that smack of blackmail and threats, saying (in my culture, for example) that you are destined to become ill, but that if you can produce $10,000 your disease can be avoided, or that the reason why your family lives in disharmony is that there have not been enough services performed in honor of your ancestors, and that if you will simply provide the organization with $30,000, your problem will be alleviated.

(3) Introducing fearful thoughts into people's minds, which I think of as a form of brainwashing. This consists mainly of stirring up dark thoughts and fears about hell.

Through such practices, some religions build up their membership and rake in large sums of money. Everything is arranged in such a way that, once people have joined that faith, they become fearful of leaving it. Proclaiming that the curse of God will fall upon people is one of the ways in which these organizations keep their members and control them.

❧ *The Appeal of Counterfeit Religions*

Deep down, all human beings are capable of distinguishing true religions from counterfeit ones if they use their own judgment and insight properly. The problem is that once they come under threat, many people lose touch with their freedom. The intense force that is projected through threatening words can paralyze people's freedom of thought and action. Although they can sense that something strange or suspicious is going on, they are unable to put up any resistance. Their lack of self-esteem and self-assurance is what gets them into trouble. They find themselves being pulled into false religions simply because they are weak-willed. As a result, such religions have spread widely.

Though it pains me to say it, I do feel that people who become caught up in counterfeit religions are operating on the same plane as the groups that have ensnared them. There is a certain point at which their own vibrations match those of the people who are throwing a net around them. People who are not susceptible to those wavelengths never get caught by them, no matter what they are told. I suppose we could just dismiss the matter by saying that it all depends on one's karma from previous lifetimes, but even so, I think people need to become more strong-minded. We can all call up the courage to live by our own convictions.

You will never be able to free yourself from misfortune and suffering if you can't get past the stage of leaving everything up to other people, or crying for help from the God that exists outside you, or submitting your will to a particular religion.

As I have mentioned in previous chapters, the God that exists outside us is the absolute law that governs the movement of the universe, but does not intervene in our individual decisions. On the other hand, the God that dwells within us is one's individual, divine self that branches out from the original light of humanity. This inner God also includes the guardian divinities and spirits who are most deeply connected with us and constantly guide us from within.

Another reason why people get caught in counterfeit religions is that they harbor an inclination to take the easy way out. This happens when people do not thoroughly know themselves. Those who get caught are very lax as far as their own lives are concerned. They lack confidence and act half-heartedly. They don't much care, one way or another, how things will turn out. Conversely, people who take a good look at themselves, seriously reflect on their personal life, and really come to grips with it cannot become ensnared by a counterfeit religion.

Even if your circumstances seem to be a steady stream of suffering, misfortune, and distress, you must never become lax where your own life is concerned. If you really put your mind to it, you can definitely rise above it all. To achieve this, you must get in touch with your essential truth. What you need is a mindset that yearns to know the truth. If you seek a way of life that is in sync with truth, you will undoubtedly find it. On the other hand, if there is no longing in your heart to find truth, you will never find it during this lifetime.

❧ Why People Balk at Truth

Here, I would like to clarify the term 'absolute truth.' Some might find my words perplexing, because many teachings and ceremonies that were previously described as the absolute truth have already spread through the world, and yet suddenly they seem to have become unnecessary.

True teachings appear when they are needed, then disappear with the passing of time. Some of these truths, having outlived their usefulness completely, have turned into 'relics' of truth. Of course, even if thousands or tens of thousands of years elapse, ultimate truths, such as the principles of love and harmony that govern the universe, do not change at all. However, if you rigidly adhere to a certain manifestation of truth, just as it was taught many thousands of years ago, you may throw modern people into confusion. The way truth is taught is bound to change with the passing of time, and truths are born anew from era to era. One great philosopher expressed it this way:

> *The phenomenal world is a place where old things are broken down and new ones are constantly being born. To cling forever to the old obstructs the birth of the new. Attachment thus impedes the natural movement of the universe. Even when the old is splendid and fine, it cannot stay exactly as it is. We must avoid attaching ourselves to the old forms of things.*[10]

Also, unlike today, there were no tape recordings available in olden times. There weren't even books that were personally written by religious teachers such as Jesus and Sakyamuni Buddha. Their words were written down later by their disciples or by people who had heard them speak. Because of this, their teachings have not always been transmitted with perfect accuracy. The writings that have been left to us were compiled from what had been verbally conveyed from person to person, based on what different people had heard. Thus, it is only natural for the truths they taught to have become somewhat distorted along the way.

In the future, the world may become more and more turbulent. Society may become more and more confused, human relationships may become more and more complicated, and people's outlooks and values may become quite different from what they once were. When you experience these kinds of changes, the question of what you, as one human being, should do to rise above it depends on your mental and spiritual attitude. It would be a mistake to complacently join a particular religion just because someone advised you to, or because you heard that there were benefits to be gained, or that it would enhance your mental and spiritual powers. On your own, you should be able to discern and confirm whether a given religion is true or counterfeit. Far from rising above their difficulties, many, many people have experienced prolonged misery and suffering simply because they joined a particular religion.

My only wish is for people to suffer less and to free themselves from their illusions. I would like them to know the truth, and to base their way of life on accurate judgment and understanding. If each and every one of us could walk the way of truth on our own initiative, there would be no need at all to join a religion.

When I see so many people in pain and misery, I cannot help thinking that something is wrong somewhere. Sooner or later, each and every one of us must awaken to our ultimate truth. We cannot be wholly relieved of our anguish if we go on being taught fallacies or partial truths and believing in them.

Ultimately, you are the only one who can truly liberate

yourself. No religion, no group, no organizational structure can do it for you. What frees you is truth—the absolute truth, and nothing else.

Although the truth has been veiled for a long time, it has now been brought nearer to us than ever before. Never has there been a period in history when the deep, divine truth has been brought so closely within the reach of humanity. The only possible hindrance, I feel, is that some of us might balk when faced with the truth of our divinity. It might seem to us that what we had previously been taught as 'truth' has been turned upside down.

In reality, though, this truth is no different from the truths of past eras. It is exactly the same truth. The only difference lies in the way it is presented. What has really happened is that the layers in which the truth has been wrapped have been peeled away, so that the unvarnished truth has become directly manifest for all to see.

❧ You Yourself are Truth

Truth is not an external entity, nor is it an organization such as a church, temple, or other religious body. Certainly, saints such as Jesus and Buddha are the very truth itself, and this is indeed the point. Truth does not originate from contrived precepts, admonitions, doctrines, prayers, or ceremonies. Truth exists in one's own self. The divine truth of the universe reveals itself through each individual human being.

For decades, centuries, and millenniums, people have been taught to offer their suffering to God through prayer, to entrust themselves to God, to rely on God and seek God. Yet, when they thought of God, they envisioned a being that existed separately from themselves. They thought of an absolute God, ruling everything from a distance.

This absolute God is the absolute law itself, and law is always law. However ardently one may wish and pray for something, the absolute law itself never changes. The absolute law cannot be expected to step in and comply with our personal requests. If we waited for the time that it would take for that to happen, humankind would never, ever be awakened. The world would remain in the same ignorant state that it is in now.

In your life, you may have been taught that you are a weak, incompetent, base, unclean, imperfect, gluttonous creature, but this is not the truth. You yourself are truth. You yourself are love, light, wisdom, infinite capability, and perfection.

You are the infinite universe. Universal truth exists majestically in each of us. All we need to do is give expression to it. All we need to do is to accept the self that is shining with love, peace, and harmony.

In the past, you may have focused too much on your powerless 'self,' your self-demeaning, imperfect 'self.' Having overemphasized your negative side, you may have ended up seeing that side as your true self. But that is a mistake. If you change your way of viewing your own mind, you will become aware that there exists another, splendid self. Just rediscover it. Little by little, keep drawing out the brilliantly shining being that is within you. In this way, you will find your outstanding self, your pure and fine self, your compassionate self and your fair-minded self. All these qualities are born from the infinite universe, and all you have to do is keep manifesting them to a greater and greater degree.

❧ *Two Sides to Your Mind*

If you have a real desire to understand the truth, the important thing is to keep shaking off the fallacies that have found their way into your thoughts. As you become more and more aware of what aspects of your beliefs have been in error, you can naturally awaken to truth.

Become aware that your true mind is the infinite universe, and declare it to yourself clearly. There is no need to hesitate, or to adhere to formalities and the fixed ideas of the past.

Your essence is perfect and infinite. It is not faulty or defective. Your words, which are replete with love, are divine words. Your thoughts, which are overflowing with wisdom, are divine thoughts. Your actions, which are filled with truth, are divine actions. Your image, which reflects grace, clarity, and beauty, is a divine image. The work of your spirit, radiating luminous energy that soothes everyone and everything around you, is divine. Wake up to the existence of this other you, the one whom you have been rejecting and restricting for such a long time. See this other you, whom you have been holding down and depriving of its freedom.

This bright side of you has been hidden from view. Most of the time, only the shadowy side has appeared on the surface. This shadowy side is the exact reverse of the bright side. You can wake up to the existence of your other mind, the one you have been shutting out for such a long time.

Let us imagine that you have been distraught with suffering, sorrow, and self-hate, that you are half-mad with hatred and jealousy, and that as a result you have ended up doing wicked things and cheating people. You have woven a web of deception and brought about the downfall of others. Though all those things might have occurred, your true self is still infinite and divine. Up to now, however, only your dark side has come to the surface.

When I say 'dark side' or 'shadowy side,' I mean the karma of a past consciousness that reveals itself in the process of fading away. That side of you has no lasting existence. Once those karmic conditions have revealed themselves and vanished, everything will take a turn for the better. There is no need to let them weigh upon you. Whatever they may consist of, they can arrive like a gentle breeze and vanish like a gentle breeze. Even if they turn into storms, typhoons, or tornadoes, they are destined to vanish, and a blue sky will appear again. There is no need to hold on to the adversity that comes your way. Just let it pass by naturally.

You need not be thrown into a panic by the storms and the typhoons. No matter how rough the waves are, deep within yourself you have the power, the wisdom, and the endless energy to endure them. Instead of being struck with fear by the scale of your adversities, you must know that the magnificent energy, ability, and wisdom to see them through lies concealed within you. All you have to do is to wield that power. All you have to do is recognize it and believe in it.

Every person is endowed with that kind of power. It is there. You must simply become aware of it.

❧ Truth is Rising to the Surface

In the past, you may have subordinated yourself to those who held worldly power yet lived a life of falsehood. Until now, such people have been able to flaunt their authority and control others, because there were plenty of weak people around to obey them. Honest people, on the other hand, have tended to live huddled up in an attitude of humility and self-effacement. Society has been so corrupt that people who live conscientiously have had a hard time getting by in this world.

From the standpoint of the unawakened ones who have been controlling you—that is to say, from the standpoint of their karmic selves—things would become very uncomfortable if you did not go on suffering. They would find it very disagreeable if you rose above the level of mediocrity and chose not to remain forever plagued by misery. They would like for you to continue being powerless, incompetent, run-of-the-mill people forever. Their karmic selves would be in trouble if you woke up to what has been happening and learned the truth. From the perspective of karma, truth is a very dangerous thing.

However, infinite wisdom and power are actively working in people who strive to elucidate the truth. We are now entering an age in which falsehoods and evils will come tumbling down, and all forms of corruption will naturally be extinguished. Everyone will emerge as a shining being.

For centuries, we have been misrepresenting ourselves. Even toward saints and sages, people could not express themselves honestly or lay their hearts bare. We have hidden, even from ourselves, the murky parts that we did not want to be known. We have kept turning our attention elsewhere, pretending not to know about our own, deeply hidden secrets.

You yourself are the only one who can honestly recognize those parts of yourself for what they are, without hiding them away. You are the only one who can understand them accurately, and recognize that they are fading away. Do not be despondent or embarrassed about them, for you are not the only one who is hiding something. It is a habit shared by all of humanity.

When we look back on history, we can definitely say this much: humanity has never stopped longing for peace, yet at the same time, it has not wanted to be delivered from its illusions. Great saints and wise people, in their efforts to set humanity free, have repeatedly disclosed the absolute truth, yet people have always ended up ignoring or nullifying the truth that was expressly shown to them.

Now, however, the time is approaching when truth cannot be nullified or ignored any longer. Each human being is progressing to a higher dimension, and each of us is approaching our infinite, divine self.

❧ Our Heartbeat and Our Breath

For we have already brushed against the absolute truth. Having come this far, there is no turning back. Our weak, faulty, powerless selves belong to the past. Even if we sometimes experience fear, unhappiness, and difficulty, our hearts need not be thrown into turmoil each time those feelings appear. We need not become obsessed by them or agonize over them, because the strength to overcome them keeps welling up within us. The wisdom that surpasses those obstacles is always surging forth, always overflowing without limit from its deep, vast, infinite source.

Now that we are nourishing the absolute truth that is within us, it is starting to bloom and grow in our hearts. Before too long, misery, pain, and frustration will have nowhere to stay. Since seeds of negativity will not be planted anymore, they will not be able to grow. None of the immense energy and power that abound within us will be used to support anything negative. The only things that will grow and bear fruit are bright thoughts of infinite happiness, infinite joy, infinite life, infinite success, and infinite prosperity. Only divinity will exist in our hearts.

Divinity is not a remote, dreamlike condition. Divinity is the life of the universe—our heartbeat and our breath.

We must know that the splendor and majesty of the universe lives within us. We must become conscious of this. Otherwise, we will perish, even before the Earth itself goes to ruin.

Once we have awakened, all human beings will safeguard the existence of our Earth. This is the solemn duty entrusted to each of us, and we must quickly become conscious of it.

🐦 Awakened People

At this point in time, there are a growing number of awakened people who are living as divine beings. They have become aware of their divinity, and are letting it show in their words and actions. Their consciousness of divinity is deepening day by day.

Most of them have stopped dragging around and reliving the sufferings of the past. Some live so positively that they can face any situation without fearing it or fleeing from it. Through their self-awareness as divine human beings, they can correctly process the karmic waves that are circling around them. Everything about them resonates divinity: they believe in their own infinite power, and they utilize their own capabilities. When misfortune, disharmony, frustration, and failure emerge from their past karmic thoughts, they surmount them all, one after another.

Whatever might happen, awakened people never flinch or

waver. They simply pour all their energy into activating their infinite, innate power as universal beings, and put all their abilities to work as they strive to rise above the karmic whirlpools.

The rapturous, joyful feeling that they experience after each whirlpool has dissipated is a thing of purity beyond words. Because they activated their own power, believed in their own divinity, rightly assessed their own thoughts and chose the means of resolving them with their own, inner resources, it is perfectly natural for them to take pride in their own trustworthiness and dauntless will. Their victory was not won because they begged for external help from God, or were propped up by other people, or bowed their heads and quashed their own convictions. They overcame adversity because they drew on their own strength and used it freely. This sense of achievement, enrichment, and victory brings with it an uplifting of the spirit and a delight of the soul that is beyond description.

People who have acquired the ability to overcome their karmic conditions with their own power never become distraught. They may be engulfed in natural disasters, the Earth may be facing destruction, and the end of humanity may be imminent, but nothing can weaken their will. Because they are deeply aware of the divinity that resides within them, they are filled with a sense of confidence and assurance that, whatever may happen, the situation will certainly get better—they will rise above it and become free from it. They are never afraid, nor do they feel any anxiety. That way of life, in itself, can be described as the consciousness of divinity.

Once your mind has freed itself of all the elements that attract disharmony, the only conditions that naturally appear are wonderful ones: happiness, prosperity, joy, success, and health. From the very outset, this has been the nature of human life. It is the original way of divinity, the original way of human beings. For human beings are the divine life of the universe, and our missions are woven into the great, natural law.

If each of us continues to be caught up in distorted or partial truths, there will be no end to our suffering and misery. That is because, in this material world, any manifestation of truth is destined to grow old, to fade, and to decompose with time. Truths, too, must renew themselves with the advance of time. The veils that have covered them must be drawn back. The sublimely high truth, the infinitely deep truth, the endlessly vast truth, the eternally shining truth dwells, just as it is, in each one of us.

Your Inner Truth is Shouting at You

I hope that each and every member of humanity will become aware of this as soon as possible, for this awareness and this awakening are what enable us to attain happiness. If we want to be cured of our illness, we can do it with our own limitless power. If we want our work to succeed, we can make it happen with our own unlimited ability. Down to the last detail, we create the world that we have envisioned.

Always living with an attitude of suffering and sadness, always letting pain recur in your heart and never feeling free is pure negligence and should not be allowed to happen. The real sin is to cover up your own light. If you are unwilling to know the truth that is within you, rejecting it instead of giving expression to it, your attitude will keep you in constant pain. For people who are overwhelmed with suffering, who cannot cope with their illness, who are anguishing under conditions of disharmony, who always fail no matter what they do, or who meet with frustrations and accidents one after another, the situation is like this: the truth within them is cascading forth and shouting at them, urging them to awaken to it at the earliest possible moment.

I hope that more and more people will attune themselves to this voice of truth and listen carefully to it. Please know that it is talking to you, trying to pry open the gate to your mind. Be as happy as you can, as soon as you can. Fill your mind with joy and gratitude. Create a life without illness, failure, despair, pain, or anguish. With your own hands, create a life that shines with freedom. You can do it. You have the power to do it. You absolutely have.

I would like you to realize that, if you recognize yourself as a divine ray of the universe, that kind of radiant, happy life can come to you immediately. Once you have been able to do this, I hope that you will let those who are still living with their illusions and anguish see how very different a human being's life can become. And I hope you will let them know that at one time you, too, used to lead the same life of suffering.

❧ Praise Your Mind

Just one change in our thinking can bring a change in our life. It is not money that changes our life, nor is it authority, fame, or talent. It is not factual knowledge, or weapons, or politics, or physical beauty. What changes our life is something that each of us possesses. It is our mind, our way of thinking. The mind that you have right now can construct a totally different way of life for you.

The mind holds immense power. It is true strength. It is all of everything. Take good care of your mind and be proud of it. It gives birth to everything, creates everything, and constructs everything. It is a mystical power, a divine power. Together, your mind and everyone else's mind can either destroy the planet or save it.

Each human mind can create struggle, discord, illness, and misery. It can also create happiness, harmony, health, peace, joy, and prosperity. It is not a question of study or skill. What matters is the mind itself. The only true power that exists is the power of the mind.

Without the mind, there would be no life and no death. The mind is life, truth, and power. A mere change in our thinking causes the whole world to change. Everything depends on the mind that exists within us. Our future depends on it. The future of our family and the future of humanity depend entirely on the mind.

Let us each take a new look at our mind. Let us thank it for its great work. Let us praise it. Let us applaud it. Let us pledge that we will manifest the divine spirit of the universe that resides within us. As soon as we possibly can, I hope that every single member of humanity will be able to carry out this pledge.

You are the Universe.

☙

First published in September 1995

CHAPTER 7

Declaring the Will
of the Universal Law

As we human beings continue to evolve, the time will come when all of us will be able to receive the messages sent from divine planes, and live according to them.

From ancient times up to the present, the divine world has been continuously emitting its precepts to all humanity. In past times, saints such as Jesus and Sakyamuni Buddha, as well as other wise people, received those subtle vibrations and conveyed them to others. Now, however, we have come to an age when all human beings can attune themselves to those divine communications.

Since everyone in the world originally came from the same divine source, each of us has naturally been provided with the same ability to receive these divine vibrations. Unfortunately though, most of us have kept that ability locked away in a far corner of our minds, where it has been almost completely forgotten.

Now, it is time for that forgotten ability to be called forth in each human heart. Humanity must soon reawaken to truth, and become newly conscious of the intuitive rays that are beaming through from our divine source.

Wherever we are, at any and all times, divine messages are always being projected where they are needed. They are sent in the form that is easiest for each person to receive and grasp firmly. They might come in a flash of inspiration, or an intuitive feeling or premonition, or an instance of clairvoyant perception, or an influx of healing power, or in all sorts of other ways. The messages are clearly transmitted to us in the ways that are easiest for us to understand.

Today, these divine communications are not coming to us by way of saints and sages, nor are they being pointed out to us by our teachers, elders, friends, or acquaintances. They are being revealed to each one of us through our very own capabilities. That is why, instead of saying that they are 'being revealed,' it would really be more accurate to say that we are 'revealing them' ourselves.

These divine messages can reach us because our true and fundamental selves are all firmly connected with the origin of the universe. Through this connection, there is a constant flow of energy moving back and forth at unconscious levels. It is through this exchange of energy that we are able to call forth the communications emitting from divine planes, and we can do it knowingly. As a result, when we wish to do something or know something, we can draw it forth and direct it as we wish.

In order to receive these divine revelations, it is necessary to understand yourself deeply and recognize that you exist in this world as one stream of universal divine life itself. And since you are the life of the universe itself, you must know that the infiniteness of the universe resides entirely within you.

Once you know this truth, it will be possible for you to change yourself. The you who used to lean on others all the time will turn into the *you* who can now make things happen wholly on your own. You yourself will be able to take charge of your own circumstances and carry everything to completion. Using the full wisdom and power that are inherent in you, you can call forth and give expression to whatever you wish.

Now is the time when the whole of humanity must become clearly aware that they have within them an infinite power source that enables them to attain solutions for everything by their own will. We have come to the moment when we must become aware of this and learn how to put it into practice. We must know it on our own, recognize it on our own, and learn it on our own. From start to finish, each of us is responsible for our own self, and for carrying our heartfelt wishes through to the very end.

❧ Real, Living Experience

When we suddenly come to a moment of crisis, there is no one outside ourselves who can take over for us. Knowledge alone will not rescue us, either. What guides us to true fulfillment is our own real, living experience. Even if your experience has been negative, unsavory, or depressing, even if it seemed to be a continuous series of humiliations and failures, your own, real experience is a precious, living teaching, and it assists you in discovering a brilliant new path.

Frustration, disappointment, loneliness, and other painful experiences may have carved themselves so deeply into your heart that there seems no way to erase them. Even so, those experiences were not without meaning. Even if they were loathsome and disgusting, even if they seemed to be the most futile experiences imaginable, they are, in fact, among your greatest assets, because they have allowed you to bring about a change in your thinking.

Every single member of humanity has endured some kind of pain or heavy burden. But, in and of themselves, those sufferings are of no lasting consequence. Their great value comes alive when they urge and guide us toward the realization of our divinity. They appeared because they were indispensable in the course of our awakening to truth. They were a process we could not avoid going through in order to perceive and recognize the communications being emitted to us from a deeper realm of existence.

Now, it is time for humanity to put an end to its suffering. We do not need to take on any additional injuries, worries, or sorrows. Through thousands of years of history, humanity has tasted all the bitterness that it needs to taste. There is nothing new to be gained from such experiences. There is no need whatsoever for the conflicts and wars to continue.

This is because each individual has already lived and relived the same stories many times. Through repeated existences, we have studied all the lessons that pain, illness, war, and genocide have to offer. We have completed our studies and earned our diplomas in misery, tragedy, and affliction. With diplomas in hand, we are now ready to step into an entirely new world—the world of the spirit.

Humanity is now beginning to recognize what has been happening. Many people are starting to become aware that they have studied all the pain and misery that they need to study. Having fully experienced the senselessness of killing their own kind again and again, they are ready to give up on it. People are now starting to feel a sense of repulsion, a sense of the absurdity of it all, along with a feeling that we must now do things differently.

We have come to a time when humanity is able to awaken to truth. We are at the moment in our evolution when we are meant to become aware of the enormity of our own capabilities and inner wisdom. Now is precisely the time for us to return to harmony with the universe. All of our mistakes must be released and left behind, to vanish forever.

❧ Nothing Exists Except Divinity

From now on, the only thing that will register in our conscious-ness is divinity—nothing else. To reach this awareness has been the purpose of our lives. When each of us has awakened to our essential, divine consciousness, the world around us will instantly be transformed and humanity's future will begin to shine.

This means that you yourself will instantly begin to shine. Through many past births and rebirths, you have instructed yourself in the ways of misfortune, sorrow, and affliction, and have completed all your studies in those areas. To continue pursuing those same subjects now would be the height of folly, now that you have your diploma in hand.

You are about to enter such an extraordinarily wonderful way of life that it thrills the emotions to think of it. And the guide who will lead you there is you—you, yourself. Everything can be found in your own mind, your true mind, the mind that accepts only what is divine. You have already awakened to truth. You have freed yourself from the rules and regimentation of the past. You have released yourself from all the old edicts and constraints that were contrived by society.

Divine inspiration is surging forth from your free mind as if from a fountain—the pure and crystal clear fountain of your life. This inner fountain of life, which you have now discovered, is so richly overflowing that no matter how much you take from it, it can never be exhausted. And so you will live abundantly each day, converting divine revelations into divine words, divine thoughts, and divine actions, giving expression to the *you* who is divine.

Finally, you will unerringly recognize that there is no real existence in this world apart from what is divine. Even if there seem to be things that are not divine, you will not accept them as such. You will treat all of them as mere stages in a process that occurs through a great universal design. You will see their great value as a series of experiences that serve to awaken humanity and inform people of their divinity. From now on, you will look at all the phenomena that pass in front of you from the standpoint of your divine consciousness.

❧ Entering 'Graduate School'

The past has completely ended. Having graduated from the 'university' of past experiences, you are able to enter 'graduate school.' By 'graduate school,' I mean the higher path that takes us ever closer to our infinite source. It is a simple path that leads us straight back to our origin. It is a path where everything goes well, everything falls perfectly into place, and everything comes together in harmony. It is a path founded on a completely different world view from the one we held in the past.

What do we study in graduate school? Day in and day out, we practice filling our thoughts with words of infinite light: *infinite love, infinite harmony, and infinite life.* This is called the 'steadfast practice of bright thinking.' Next, we concentrate on actions filled with thankfulness to the Earth and the environment. While walking, working, bathing, and preparing and eating our meals, we make it a habit to cherish and respect all things as we think or say, 'Thank you, dear earth; thank you, dear water; thank you dear air, and dear food.'[11] We learn to practice daily thankfulness to each cell that composes our physical bodies and to all things that support and sustain our lives.

Once we have filled our thoughts with gratitude and light, it becomes possible for us to conceive of our own infinite light, so we then try declaring to ourselves, 'I am an infinite being,' or 'I am the Universe,' or 'I am one with the Universe.'[12] After that, we can embark on practices such as the Universal *INs*, and mandalas of gratitude and light.[13]

As we apply ourselves to these practices day by day, their effects start to pervade every aspect of our lives, drawing us closer and closer to our original, divine image. Our study program does not offer classes in misfortune, sorrow, or affliction. The only course available is in our divinity. And as we continue to manifest the divine conditions that we are outlining with our thoughts, our infinite wisdom reveals itself more and more in the forms of inspiration, intuitive awareness, healing energy, and in a wealth of other ways.

In graduate school, everything that we think and imagine works toward the positive. All our efforts are focused on learning to bring out our infinite capabilities—wisdom, prosperity, success, happiness, and peace—and converting them to action. We reject everything that is negative. No negative words are spoken, no negative thoughts are emitted, and no negative actions are performed. No negative concepts receive any recognition at all.

The only thing that we recognize is our universal divine consciousness, and our lives expand outward from that point. Divine consciousness is what keeps guiding us toward the light, toward an endless, infinitely peaceful and dynamic life.

Since graduate school is made up entirely of people with this frame of mind, nothing negative exists there. Having already graduated from the school of negative thoughts, words, and actions, everyone's thoughts are positive, and everyone lives in a positive world.

Positive thoughts, words, and actions can give rise only to positive results. That is why there exists no failure, fear, or illness, nor is there any unhappiness, frustration, or setback. There cannot be even the faintest element of struggle, hatred, or anger in this world, as all traces of them have already vanished from each person's heart. There is no dissatisfaction, accusation, or jealousy. There is no competitiveness or conflict. However you might examine your heart in search of it, you will find no more anger or enmity. Selfish cravings cannot arise. However closely you may observe yourself, you will find nothing of the sort within you, nothing at all.

No, nothing at all, even though your heart may once have been seething with indignation and animosity, even though you may once have been beaten down by fear, anguish, and sorrow, or buffeted by illness, accidents, and disasters. In those days, others may have urged you to search deep within and recognize your divine self. But though you kept trying, you could not find divinity in your heart.

Now, the situation has reversed itself. However you may search your heart for anger, there is no anger to be found. However hard you may look, there is no sadness, no falseness, no deception at all. There is nothing but consciousness of divinity. There is nothing but positive thoughts and feelings. Have you noticed it? Though you are still exactly the same individual as before, your consciousness now recognizes only what is divine.

❧ Declaring the Will of the Universal Law

How relaxed you are now! How free! The images that appear in your mind contain absolutely no trace of uneasiness or doubt. You are always thinking that things will go well, that the situation will improve, that people's ills will be eased. You are always thinking: 'We are sure to succeed! It will definitely happen!' Your consciousness is filled with positive thoughts and feelings like these, and nothing else. Skepticism does not arise. You no longer even need to put forth the effort to strike out dark thoughts with bright ones.

You have progressed enormously. You have awakened to a great degree. You might even wonder if this is really you at all. This is how it feels to awaken to truth. Everything expands and develops according to your own will. Everything is guided to fruition. Everything goes smoothly, just as you intended it to. Everything crystallizes perfectly. And during the process, you spontaneously become conscious of the divine revelations that are emerging in your mind. At the moment when intuition starts to shimmer, you are already gearing yourself to action.

For example, if you hesitate for a moment on whether to turn left or right, a divine revelation arrives and you intuitively choose to go right. Or, when a hidden obstacle lies ahead of you, a divinely inspired thought reveals itself in your mind and, spurred on by a premonition, you devise a marvelous way to circumvent it.

As you proceed along the path you have envisioned, there might be a serious illness in store. Yet, as your natural healing power comes through, you are quickly able to set it right. Aligning yourself with the laws of nature, you rise above it beautifully.

This is because there is nothing in your mind but positive thoughts, such as 'I am an infinite being,' 'Everything will come into harmony,' 'Everything will absolutely improve,' and 'Everything will fall into place.' Through the light vibrations being received, your inner powers are fully activated, and you call forth infinite, divine energy. With your limitless wisdom and capabilities fully in motion, you are able to give perfect expression to the oneness of life.

Those who attend this graduate school are people who, no matter what, recognize nothing except divinity, or else are striving to. Whatever might happen around them, they can see it through with these thoughts of infinite light: 'Everything will absolutely get better! Infinite wisdom! Infinite capability!' They can accept divine messages, assimilate them, and give expression to them to a very great extent. They clearly understand what truth is. They know that truth already exists, and is not something that needs to be created, planned, or investigated.

Truth is you, yourself. You are truth. The *you* who exists here and now, and is divine, is truth. Truth is not something apart from you, nor can you go out and look for it. It cannot be manufactured or invented, either. It simply exists where you are.

If you assume that truth exists within you, and that you yourself are truth, you will naturally conclude that there is no power in this world that can defeat you. Even if you meet with a temporary setback, as long as you keep manifesting truth, there can be no power strong enough to repress it. On the other hand, if you keep cutting yourself off from truth, creating a false power that works against you and assigning credibility to it, you will end up letting yourself be controlled by it. In turning away from truth, you are constructing all sorts of obstacles in front of you.

Once you recognize this, you will be able to freely and confidently manifest all sorts of things, without any uneasiness, fear, or doubt. You can do it by constantly declaring to yourself, 'Everything will definitely get better! I am one with the Universe!'

The declaration 'Everything will definitely improve!' or 'Everything will certainly get better!' applies not just to you alone. It reaches everything that lives and exists. When you make this declaration, it is like saying, 'Everyone and everything, listen well: everything will turn out perfectly; everything will achieve completion; everything will find harmony.' These positive declarations are intended for all beings that live in this great universe.

This means that animals, plants, and other organisms, minerals, water, mountains, the earth, and everything that exists in it and around it will, without fail, achieve great harmony. These words embody the universal truth that all forms of life are destined to cherish one another, help and encourage one another, love one another, and bring happiness to one another as they progress toward great harmony.

The infinite spirit of the universe is speaking to us with the energy of divine words. Originally, words carry a divine spirit, and are a source of light, vibration, and truth.[14] This is why I feel that it is an excellent thing to keep saying the words

'Everything will definitely get better!' along with the declaration 'I am one with the Universe.'

❧ Declaring Peace for Everything in Existence

As we repeat the declaration 'I am one with the Universe' or 'I am the Universe' to ourselves, our consciousness will be uplifted and purified until it reaches a state of divinity. Voicing this declaration enables us to reach a state that transcends all dichotomies, such as life versus death, good versus bad, and happiness versus unhappiness.

Once these dichotomies have been surpassed, our infinite, divine consciousness can build a world based on light alone, where everything moves in peace and harmony. Since our infinite, divine consciousness desires peace and blessings for everything in existence, the declaration 'I am one with the Universe' is actually directed at everything in existence. It is like saying to all living things, ourselves included, that everything will definitely improve. Then, everything in creation, having felt the resonance of our declaration, will be able to move toward the positive, toward harmony and peace.

'Everything will definitely get better!' This declaration contains a vast and profound meaning. While it extends to all living things in this world, it simultaneously permeates all the thoughts and emotions, anguish and illness that twine round the physical consciousness, as well as all the circumstances that crop up in a person's life.

This declaration has precisely the same meaning as the words 'May peace prevail on Earth.' 'May peace prevail on Earth' is a wish and a prayer for the peace and happiness of everything on Earth, including our own peace and happiness

108

as individuals. When we focus on these words, within our consciousness there is an exchange of energy among all living things, ourselves included, so that all things can achieve harmony with one another.

All of us intuitively know that our individual lives could never exist cut off from others. Each life is capable of living because it is sustained and supported by all other lives. The first thing we need to know is that we can live because we are enlivened by everything in existence. Consequently, the words 'May peace prevail on Earth' naturally serve as a vehicle for humanity to speak to everything in creation. Through these words, the resonance of the universal divine will, through which all things achieve peace, sends shining life to everything that is.

By constantly receiving and transmitting this universal divine energy, we have been undergoing an enormous change of consciousness. All our thoughts are turning into divine thoughts; all our words are turning into divine words; all our behavior is becoming divine. We are coming to recognize no reality other than what is divine. We are experiencing the truth that in ourselves, and in all living things, there is no consciousness other than divine consciousness.

What Our True Selves are Striving for

From now on, we will go on receiving divine revelations and holding them up for humanity to see. It is important for us to let the beauty and radiance of our divinity be perceived by others, through actions filled with dignity and words that abound with love and affection. Divine revelations will scintillate through our thoughts, and as we freely command all our circumstances, our thoughts will find expression in the tangible world. This is, after all, what we are living for—what our true selves are striving for.

Each of us can choose our own way of sending bright sparks of truth to humanity. Each in our own way, let us foster the development of more and more pioneers who will pave the way for everyone to awaken to their divinity.

Once enough people have awakened, this world will begin to change. The divinely inspired words, thoughts, and actions of these pioneers, along with the powerful energy of their wishes and prayers for world peace, will produce a huge transformation in world society.

There is no need to rush. There is no need to feel burdened or duty-bound. Everything will occur spontaneously, when the time is right. The truth will smoothly and naturally flow into our lives and spread to others. People who are meant to join in the early stages of this process will naturally come forth of their own accord.

In each moment of every day, let us enhance our consciousness of divinity by one more step. The only effort we need to make is to brighten and uplift ourselves, revealing the divinity that is within, so that when others see us, they will feel that they have seen the light of love itself.

After awakening to truth, each human being is destined to become a rescuer of the planet. When a million people have awakened, it means that a million rescuers have appeared. Each of us is a rescuer who will bring true peace to humanity. How awe-inspiring it is to live for such a purpose! It almost seems too good to be true that each of us is actually a rescuer of humanity!

Actually, there should be nothing surprising about it. Once

we have awakened to our infinite truth, it is only natural for us to emit life-giving, renewing energy to everyone and everything on Earth. Since we were born for this purpose, shall we not devote ourselves to it for as long as we are here? Shall we not always live our lives with this noble purpose in mind?

This is not something to be thought of as taxing or difficult, not in the least. We are already doing a portion of the work now. We do it each time we wish or pray for peace on earth. We do it each time we affirm our divinity, or perform the universal *INs*, or send out bright words, or express our gratitude to the earth and the environment. If this is not the role of a rescuer of the Earth, I wonder what is? Thanks to activities like these, the task of saving the planet is already in progress.

What wonderful, shining lives we are leading! For the remainder of our time here on Earth, let us ignite all our life-energy for the happiness of humanity. Then, when our work has been completed, we will leave with no regrets, ascending to a light-filled plane where our true selves are already living. Let us do our best each day until our consciousness has fully entered that joyful state.

You are the Universe.

First published in November 1995

Fading Away—May Peace Prevail on Earth

A Teaching of Absolute Love and Forgiveness

These days, I have been explaining things to people in this way:

Everything that takes shape in the form of sickness, poverty, and so on is a manifestation of karma (thoughts, words, and actions from a past consciousness), appearing at the moment when it is supposed to vanish away. Therefore, when illness, financial problems, or other such circumstances arise in your life, I do not recommend that you search for the hidden causes behind them by digging up the mistaken attitudes that you may have held in the past. Just think that all this suffering is occurring in the process of fading away, and that it will absolutely vanish into nothingness. Then, once it has entirely disappeared, your original, infinite light will shine through and a truly wonderful world will take shape around you.

So, all you need to do is to think, with your whole being, that all those unpleasant experiences are fading away, and to feel gratitude toward the infinite love and protection of the universe. And a really effective way to do this is with the words, 'Fading away—May peace prevail on Earth.' If you continue to practice this method wholeheartedly, without giving up, you can rest assured that things will most definitely turn out well.

This is a teaching of complete entrustment—absolute trust in the divine. It is a teaching of unconditional love and forgiveness, recognizing not even one speck of evil in the true nature of a human being. If you want to offer people a sure, true teaching on the perfect nature of a human being, tell them about this. This in itself is enough.

from *Daily Meditations* by Masahisa Goi, 1980

Words of Happiness and Light

Here is a method for focusing only on your inner light. When a dark thought crosses your mind, counter it with a bright thought like 'I am light!' Whenever a pessimistic feeling surrounds you, pierce through it with the positive energy of words like 'infinite improvement!' From morning till night, as much as you can, create a shining life with words like 'I am love! I am harmony! Infinite power! May peace prevail on Earth!'

Here are some examples:

I am Love	I am Happiness
I am Harmony	I am Radiance
I am Peace	I am Talent
I am Light	I am Energy
I am Power	I am Potential
I am Wisdom	I am Ability
I am Life	I am Success

I am Health

I am Dignity

I am Vitality

I am Courage

I am Creativity

I am Progress

I am Originality

I am Betterment

I am Development

I am Strength

I am Growth

I am Intuition

I am Gratitude

I am Innocence

I am Joy

I am Hope

I am Beauty

I am Inspiration

I am Youth

I am Clarity

I am Good

I am Tranquility

I am Sincerity

I am Freedom

I am Purity

I am Grace

I am Brightness

I am Stillness

I am Gentleness

I am Abundance

I am Generosity

I am Integrity

I am Serenity

I am Bliss

I am Oneness

You can use this space to write your favorite bright words or create new ones:

_____

_____

_____

_____

_____

_____

_____

_____

_____

_____

_____

_____

_____

_____

_____

_____

_____

_____

_____

_____

Gratitude to
the World of Nature

GRATITUDE TO THE EARTH

My feet touched the earth. Accepting them warmly, the earth embraced my soul. I walked on the earth in silence, and the earth was in peace.

Always, the earth welcomes us tenderly, without uttering a word. Always, the earth embraces us in silence. Even if trodden upon, hurt, or polluted, the earth never tries to say anything, never tries to take revenge. The earth only gives. In heartfelt gratitude, I touch the earth and become as the earth. Oh, beloved earth—on behalf of all humanity, I thank you.

—Masami Saionji

When you have some extra space in your mind, try writing your own expressions of gratitude to nature, either on the following pages or on a separate sheet.

GRATITUDE TO THE SEA

_____

_____

_____

_____

_____

_____

_____

                                    _____

                                    (your name)

GRATITUDE TO THE EARTH

_____

_____

_____

_____

_____

_____

_____

                                    _____

                                    (your name)

GRATITUDE TO MOUNTAINS

_____

_____

_____

_____

_____

_____

_____

_____

(your name)

GRATITUDE TO ANIMALS

_____

_____

_____

_____

_____

_____

_____

_____

(your name)

GRATITUDE TO PLANTS

_____

_____

_____

_____

_____

_____

_____

_____

(your name)

GRATITUDE TO MINERALS

_____

_____

_____

_____

_____

_____

_____

_____

(your name)

GRATITUDE TO WATER

_____

_____

_____

_____

_____

_____

_____

_____

(your name)

GRATITUDE TO FOOD

_____

_____

_____

_____

_____

_____

_____

_____

(your name)

GRATITUDE TO MY PHYSICAL BODY

_____

_____

_____

_____

_____

_____

_____

_____

(your name)

GRATITUDE TO AIR

_____

_____

_____

_____

_____

_____

_____

_____

(your name)

GRATITUDE TO THE SUN

_____

_____

_____

_____

_____

_____

_____

(your name)

GRATITUDE TO HEAVENLY PHENOMENA
(rain, wind, snow, clouds, skies, planets, stars...)

_____

_____

_____

_____

_____

_____

_____

(your name)

Interview with Masami Saionji
Questions and Answers about the Universal IN for the Self

Since it was first introduced by Masami Saionji in 1994, the Universal IN for the self has been embraced by people throughout the world. In a special interview, Ms. Saionji answers some of the questions people have been asking about this IN.

Q: First, would you explain why we do the Universal IN for the self?

A: In the beginning, human beings existed within the universal law. Everything was perfect. Everything was in great harmony. Then, human beings assumed their individual roles and came down to the earthly plane, to work and to create something.

But after a long, long time had passed, human beings began to separate themselves from the universal law. They forgot their original selves. Now, it's time for human beings to wake up and remember their original selves.

What is the original self? The original self is life itself, bright and infinitely free. It is everything in the universe. It is the life of the universe.

We human beings were born from the universal source and we are exactly like the universal source—just like parent and child. The universal source is the parent and a human being is the child. When we do the Universal *IN*, we start to wake up and remember this. We remember who we really are. That's what it means to awaken to our original self.

The universe is made from energy. Everything is energy, or vibration. Words are energy. Thoughts are also energy. Actions are energy, too. When we speak negative words, that negative energy brings negative effects. When we have a negative way of thinking, our negative words vibrate negative energy to the people around us. In exactly the same way, if we speak positive, true words, our words make people happy, encouraging and brightening them.

The *IN* is also a vibration—a very strong vibration. Each of the *IN*'s movements connects us directly with the universal law, so they enable us to receive a very wonderful, powerful, infinite energy. That's why, when you do the *IN*, you can transform yourself. You remember your original self, what kind of purpose your original self has, and what kinds of things you need to keep in mind.

As we are forming the *IN*, we make the sounds '*wa-re-so-ku-ka-mi-na-ri*.' These sounds carry the vibration of 'I am one with the Universe,' or 'I am an infinite being.' Nowadays, many people don't believe that they are infinite, universal beings. But when you believe that you are a universal being, you spontaneously know and experience your oneness with other people, with nature, and with everything in creation. You know and experience the reality that everything is one being, one life.

If you feel and understand that everything in creation is in oneness, you can transform yourself. By that, I mean you can change your habits. If you have a habit of complaining, or of feeling sad, unhappy, or jealous, you can change that kind of habit.

Why do people get negative feelings in the first place? It's because they have been thinking that they are not one with others. They always feel some kind of separation. But when we do the *IN*, we feel oneness.

The *IN* holds a deep meaning. Each movement has a truth—a true meaning. Even if people haven't studied much about the *IN*, once they start doing it, step by step they naturally awaken to their original self.

When I received this *IN* from the universal law, the vibrations from the universal source told me that whenever people do this *IN*, the effect will appear for sure. The *IN* has a much stronger effect than any words, thoughts, or actions.

Q: How do we form the IN?

A: The most basic movement is to make a circle with your thumb and index finger. This circle always means 'perfect.' The right hand means 'plus' (+) and the left hand means 'minus' (−).

In this world, there are always plus (+) and minus (−) energies. If there were only one kind of energy, there would never be any activity. No work. No actions. Just stillness. No movement. Nothing would be created. That's why we have plus (+) and minus (−) energies. Plus (+) and minus (−) energies combine and interact with each other. Both kinds of energy are in our bodies.

Q: What is the meaning of each movement?

A: Each movement has a deep and vast meaning, and there are various ways of explaining it. I will try to give you a simple explanation that gives you a sense of the dignity, truth, and immense power of the *IN*.

With each movement, we make a sound at the same time. As we do this, we naturally exhale. When the movement is over, we inhale. We never inhale until the movement is finished.

If it's difficult for you to continue making a sound until the very end of the movement, it's no problem. Just make sure that you don't inhale until the movement is over.

The first sound that we make is 'uu.' (It sounds like the 'oo' in 'cool' or 'pool.') Or, if you like, instead of saying 'uu,' you can keep your mouth closed and make a humming sound, like this: 'mmm.'

Q: What if, for physical reasons, we cannot make the sounds?

A: In that case, just do your best and focus your mind on what the correct sound would be like.

Q: What if, for physical reasons, we cannot make the movements?

A: Even if you are bedridden, or have lost some fingers or limbs, you can still do the *IN* in your mind. Just try your best to form an exact, correct image of the movement through your imagination. Regardless of what condition your physical body is in, your spiritual body is complete and perfect. Your spiritual body will perform the *IN* just as you envision it in your mind.

Now, let's begin. Before you start, make a short declaration, such as 'I am an infinite being,' or 'I am a divine being,' or 'I am (one with) the Universe.' Or, instead of making this declaration in English (or another language), you can simply use the international sounds *'wa-re-so-ku-ka-mi-na-ri,'* all in sequence. After that, start the movements. I'll give you the meaning for each movement, and tell you which sound goes with it. (You can find the illustrations starting on page 140.) The first movement goes with the sound 'uu,' the second movement also goes with the sound 'uu,' the third movement goes with the sound 'wa,' and so on.

'uu' (while exhaling)
I am one with the universe. I receive infinite life and energy from the source of the universe...
(now inhale)

'uu' (while exhaling)
...and bring it into my body through this spot in my forehead, and let it travel through each cell of my body.
(now inhale)

'wa' (while exhaling)
My original self is the truth and light of the universe.
(now inhale)

'uu' (while exhaling)
My original self came down to Earth and manifested my divinity to all human beings and everything in creation.
(now inhale)

're' (while exhaling)
While I live on Earth, I am perfectly one with the universe—infinite light and harmony.
(now inhale)

'so' (while exhaling)
I am one with everything in nature: earth, air, water, the sun, mountains, rivers, rocks, oceans, and stars.
(now inhale)

'ku' (while exhaling)
I am one with everything in creation: animals, plants, and all living things.
(now inhale)

'ka' (while exhaling)
I send infinite gratitude to everything in creation and all human beings. Infinite joy, infinite wisdom, infinite light, infinite life...
(now inhale)

'mi' (while exhaling)
I send infinite gratitude to everything in nature. Infinite majesty, infinite dignity, infinite beauty, infinite joy, infinite life...
(now inhale)

'na' (while exhaling)
I embrace and uplift everything in nature and creation to heaven while receiving infinite energy from the universe...
(now inhale)

'ri' (while exhaling)

...and send all gratitude to the source of the universal law.
(now inhale)

(Now, hold your breath during the final strokes)
All my mistaken words, thoughts and actions from the past are forgiven and have vanished. ⇩

My infinite self has appeared. ⇧
(return your hands to the starting position, then exhale.

That's all. I think that some of our readers may already know how the movements are done. If they don't know, they can start practicing right now with the illustrations (starting on page 140). I would like for everyone on the planet to have a chance to learn this *IN*.

Q: Thank you. What can we do if we want to form the IN *but there are people nearby and we do not wish to do the* IN *in front of them?*

A: In that situation, without calling attention to yourself, you can form the *IN* in your mind while sitting or standing quietly where you are. Your spiritual body will perform the *IN* perfectly, as I mentioned earlier, and it will definitely work.

Q: We have heard that it's especially effective to do the IN *when we are out in nature. Why is that so?*

A: Through harmful words, thoughts, and actions, human beings have attacked the energy fields of animals, plants, and everything in nature. When we do the *INs*, we restore the energy that was interfered with. Refreshed by this new, pure energy, animals, plants, and everything in nature can recover their inherent power of self-healing.

Q: What can we do if we find it hard to go out into nature?

A: If you don't have an opportunity to go out in nature but want to revitalize nature through the *IN*, form an image in your mind of the animals, plants, water, mountains, or other living things that you want to send energy to. Then perform the *IN* while keeping that image in your mind.

Q: What should we do if we are out in nature but do not feel comfortable about doing the IN *because there are people around?*

A: In that case, you can perform the *IN* in your mind while sitting or standing in front of a tree, or a waterfall, or some flowers, or wherever you might be. It will definitely work, as I mentioned earlier.

Q: We have heard you say that it's good to have a specific purpose in mind when we do the IN. *Why is that?*

A: If you have a specific, well-meaning purpose in mind, it helps you to concentrate. Then, the energy of the *IN* will be focused on your goal and the *IN*'s effects will be clearly recognized. As you continue to recognize the effectiveness of the *IN*, your confidence will grow step by step, and this will encourage you to do the *IN* more often and more sincerely. As a result, the immense power of the *IN* can be demonstrated more fully. On the other hand, if your feelings are vague when you do the *IN*, the effects may also seem vague.

Q: Why is it important for us to make the sounds 'wa-re-so-ku-ka-mi-na-ri' before we start doing the IN *and also while we are doing it?*

A: These sounds hold a very powerful, harmonizing reso-nance. When we make these sounds, we attune our physical and mental vibrations to the pure energy of the *IN*. This refines and harmonizes all our cells, allowing us to perform the *IN* more beautifully and accurately.

Q: Some people have said that they would like to say the words 'I am the Universe' or 'I am an infinite, divine being,' but hesitate because their daily words, thoughts, and actions are not so harmonious.

A: The important point here is to distinguish between the true, infinite self and the superficial self that gets caught up in disharmony and emotionalism. When you say these words, it is not your superficial self that is talking. It is your infinite, divine self. Your divine self is speaking and creating a pure, sparkling atmosphere where you are. If you remember this, you should be able to say the words.

Q: Many people have asked who first thought up the Universal IN.

A: This *IN* was not devised through the human thought processes. It was conveyed to Earth from the source of the uni-versal law, so that human beings could awaken to their divini-ty and safely progress through the 21st century.

Q: We have learned that you were the first person to receive this IN *from the universal source. Some people are wondering how you were able to do this.*

A: Everyone has the power to receive the precepts of the universal law. At present, though, the Earth is engulfed in waves of disharmony, just like the rough waves on the ocean during a storm. Because of these rough waves, people cannot easily tune in to the delicate vibrations coming from the universal source.

Goi Sensei[15] wanted me to be able to do this, so he began training me for it when I was about twenty years old. There were many phases to this training, which I will describe in more detail when I write my autobiography. It entailed keeping my mind perfectly calm and steady in any situation, no matter what. Even after he left this world (in 1980), Goi Sensei continued training me from the world of the universal source.

The training has been both physical and mental, and it still continues today. Most people who know me are aware of my most recent assignments, which have included praying or meditating for eight hours a day for about three months at a time. These assignments have been carried out in several places—in North America, Europe, Asia, and so on. The content of the prayer or meditation is very deep and multi-faceted, and it cannot really be described with ordinary language. However, I can say that it includes learning a variety of *INs*, and it also involves purifying disharmony in the country or continent where I am. In doing these assignments, I have become more and more finely attuned to the vibrations coming from the universal source, and that's why I could receive this *IN* when it was conveyed to Earth on July 24, 1994.

You could think of it this way. Imagine that you want to tune in to a very important program on your radio, but when you turn the dial, all you can hear is static. Yet, if a person's ear is extremely well trained, they can hear the programs that are being transmitted, even through the static. My perception is something like this.

Incidentally, it may sound as if I went through this training all alone, and in a sense that is true. But thanks to the many people around the world who were intently praying for world peace, the 'static' became much lighter, and this made it possible for me to carry on my training successfully. I always feel grateful to those people.

The next point I would like to make is that once I received this *IN*, it became easier for other people to receive it. Let me explain this with another example. Suppose you want to go to the mountain, but you are surrounded by bushes growing so thick and so high that you cannot see where the mountain is or how to get to it. Yet, if just one person can clear a path to the mountain, it becomes much easier for other people to go there. As more and more people walk along the path, the path gets wider. Then, greater numbers of people can easily go to the mountain. This can be compared to my job. My job was to clear a path to the mountain.

Q: *When you received the IN from the universal source, how did it appear? Did you see someone performing the IN, or did you feel the movements through your body?*

A: It was more like feeling the movements through my body. When I meditated and received the *IN* from the universal law, I never saw anyone performing the movements. If I had to compare it to something, I'd say it's like a movie in which all the scenes appear in front of me all at once, in the space of an instant. It's somewhat like the workings of a computer, or the internet—very large-scale, yet very precise. Everything appears vividly and in great detail. Everything is perfectly clear.

One more thing. Unlike a movie, it's not a two-dimensional or even a three-dimensional image. It's four-dimensional. By 'four-dimensional,' I mean that you don't view it from just one side and one point in time. You see it from all directions—from above, from the front, from the sides, and from the interior—all at once, instantly and with perfect clarity.

You may ask, how can you convey something like that, which appears perfectly and completely within a split second, using the words of this three-dimensional world? If you want to depict a three-dimensional figure on a flat, two-dimensional surface, like a piece of paper, you can do it with dotted lines and so forth, but it's much more difficult to describe the *IN* in terms of our present-day world. To describe it, I have to divide the oneness of the *IN* into several parts—such as hand movements, eye movements, breathing, and so on. Then all those parts have to be recombined into one.

When people watch me doing the *IN*, they can only see me from one perspective. If they are sitting in front of me, they cannot see my back, or the back of my hand. They cannot feel my breathing. Yet correct breathing is very, very important. That's why I always ask people to breathe slowly.

If people could perform the *IN* with perfect precision, their bodies would be in perfect harmony and their illnesses would disappear immediately—but it takes a lot of practice to do this. And I am happy to say that people are getting better and better at it.

Q: Would you explain more about what it's like to observe the IN *all in one moment? It's not like seeing with the eyes, you said.*

A: That's right. It's not visual. It's beyond the visual. When you 'see' from a four-dimensional perspective, you are not confined to one spot. You can be everywhere, instantly. There are no barriers of distance or time.

Try imagining, for example, that you are looking at a building—say a hospital—from a four-dimensional perspective. What you see is more than just the outside of the building. You see each patient in each room. You understand the state of each person's health. You know which ones will be discharged from the hospital, and which ones will pass away while they are there. You discern that this patient is in a good mood, that one misses her family, and so on. All this is clear to you in an instant. This may give you some idea of what it's like to have a four-dimensional perspective.

When I see someone doing the *IN*, I understand the activity of all their internal systems, their blood vessels, bones, muscles, internal organs, and all their cells, in perfect detail. I perceive their cells moving, working, and creating, and I can instantly see how the *IN* influences each of their cells and their genes. I can 'see' the energy vividly at work. This is why I can clearly state that the *IN* is a perfect method for creating harmony.

Q: Is that why you say that the IN *belongs to the world of science?*

A: Yes. I say so because, seen from a fourth-dimensional world, the evidence is clear and the result is verified. There is nothing vague or subjective about it. In the fourth dimension, every part of the whole is clearly discerned. I am completely sure of why people do the *IN*, and of how its energy harmonizes and activates all the cells of the body. By 'activate,' I mean 'awaken.' The *IN* awakens each cell to its innate, infinite capability.

Even if the *IN* seems complicated or hard to learn, I would like to suggest that you try it. You can just practice part of it if you like. Also, I'd like to recommend that you try repeating the syllables that go with it—*wa-re-so-ku-ka-mi-na-ri*—whenever you have time. From minute to minute, in whatever ways we can, we human beings have to keep trying to uplift ourselves and awaken to our inner, infinite selves.

Q: On behalf of our readers, we would like to thank you for this valuable interview.

A: The pleasure is mine, and I hope that more and more people will be able to experience the wonderful effects of this *IN*.

INTRODUCING THE UNIVERSAL *IN* FOR HUMANITY

On May 19, 1996, Ms. Saionji received a second *IN*, the Universal *IN* for humanity. A year later, this *IN* was introduced to the public.

Whereas the Universal *IN* for the self works for the awakening of the individual, the Universal *IN* for humanity works for the purification and awakening of humanity as a whole. Anyone who wishes to learn and perform this *IN* may do so, regardless of whether they have learned the Universal *IN* for the self. In fact, it is now Ms. Saionji's wish that people give priority to learning the Universal *IN* for humanity, as it is more urgently needed at this point in time. As with the Universal *IN* for the self, the only requirement for learning the *IN* is that one understand its meaning.

Instructions for how to perform both *IN*s follow in Appendix V.

How to Form the
Universal IN for the Self

Before you start, say: *Wa-re-so-ku-ka-mi-na-ri*
(I am one with the Universe)

1   Starting position: The *IN* of Great Harmony

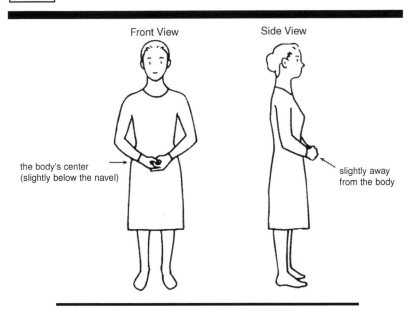

Front View   Side View

the body's center
(slightly below the navel)

slightly away
from the body

How to form the *IN* of Great Harmony

1. Make circles by joining the tips of the forefingers and thumbs.

2. Link the circles together.

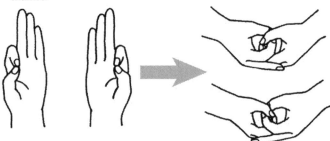

The palms face up.
Either hand can be on top.

With the hands in the starting position, begin to lift them from the body's center. While making the sound 'uu,' keep the circles linked and extend the remaining fingers. Lift the hands in a curving motion until they are level with the eyes.

make the sound

'uu'

Front View   Side View

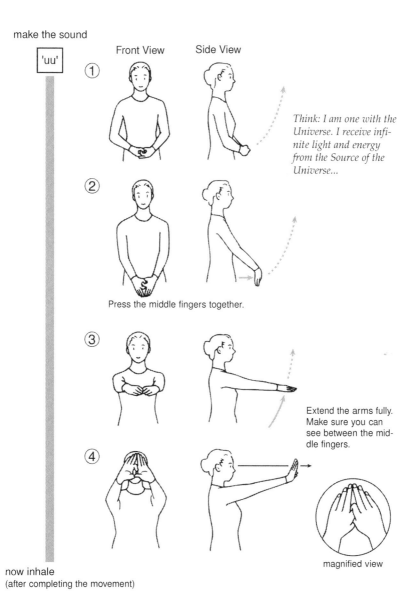

Think: I am one with the Universe. I receive infinite light and energy from the Source of the Universe...

Press the middle fingers together.

Extend the arms fully. Make sure you can see between the middle fingers.

magnified view

now inhale
(after completing the movement)

3 While making the sound 'uu,' gently bring the hands toward the face. While doing this, release the linked circles and cross the right hand fingers in front of the left hand fingers, the palms facing you. Touch the fingers to the forehead once, then extend them outward a little.

make the sound

'uu'

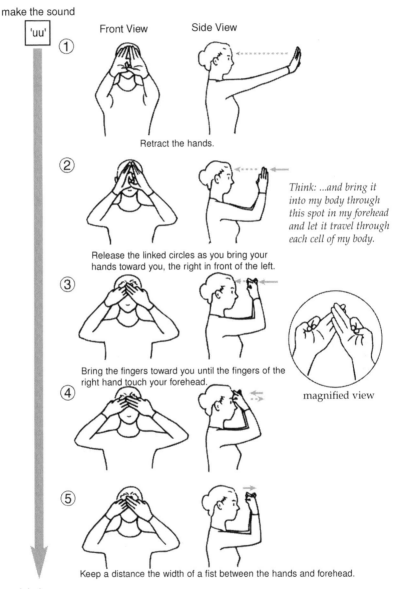

Front View   Side View

① Retract the hands.

② Release the linked circles as you bring your hands toward you, the right in front of the left.

Think: ...and bring it into my body through this spot in my forehead and let it travel through each cell of my body.

③ Bring the fingers toward you until the fingers of the right hand touch your forehead.

magnified view

④

⑤ Keep a distance the width of a fist between the hands and forehead.

now inhale
(after completing the movement)

142

4

While making the sound 'wa,' bring the right hand down in a circular motion toward the left, moving round and returning full circle. (From your point of view the circle will be counter-clockwise).

make the sound

'wa'

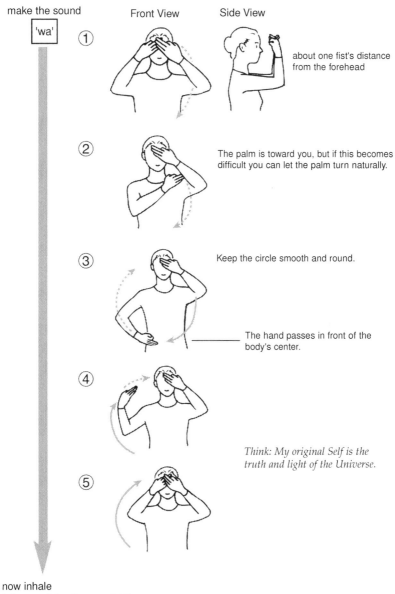

Front View   Side View

① about one fist's distance from the forehead

② The palm is toward you, but if this becomes difficult you can let the palm turn naturally.

③ Keep the circle smooth and round.

The hand passes in front of the body's center.

④

Think: My original Self is the truth and light of the Universe.

⑤

now inhale
(after completing the movement)

While again making the sound 'uu,' lower the hands, starting from in front of the forehead. While lowering the hands, again link the two circles formed by the forefingers and thumbs. Then stretch the hands out from the body's center and bring them back again.

make the sound
'uu'

Front View   Side View

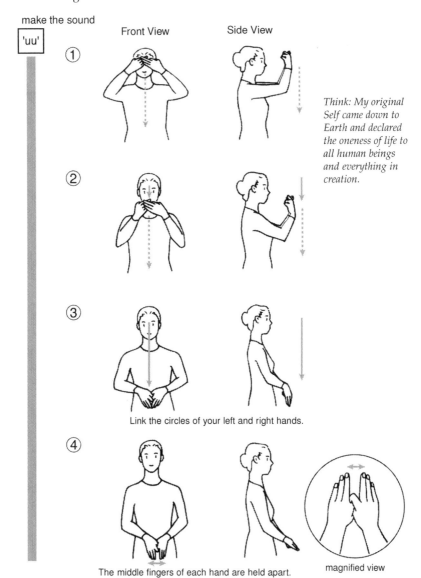

Think: My original Self came down to Earth and declared the oneness of life to all human beings and everything in creation.

Link the circles of your left and right hands.

The middle fingers of each hand are held apart.

magnified view

(continued on next page)

(continued from the previous page)

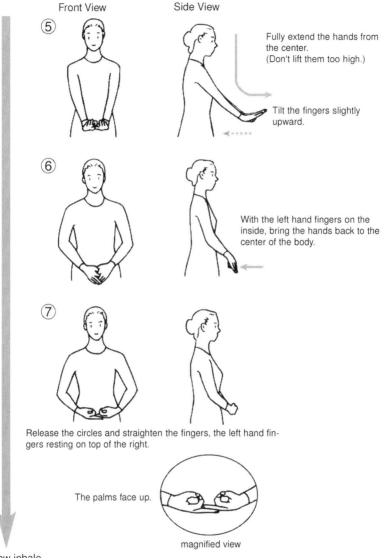

Front View   Side View

⑤ Fully extend the hands from the center.
(Don't lift them too high.)

Tilt the fingers slightly upward.

⑥ With the left hand fingers on the inside, bring the hands back to the center of the body.

⑦ Release the circles and straighten the fingers, the left hand fingers resting on top of the right.

The palms face up.

magnified view

now inhale
(after completing the movement)

6 While making the sound 're,' bring the left hand up to the right and around in a circular motion in front of the body. End the movement by touching the tips of the middle fingers together.

make the sound

'**re**'

Front View

Think: While I live on Earth, I am perfectly one with the Universe—Infinite Light and Harmony.

① ——— center of the body

② With the palm facing in, make a circle.

③ ——— The hand passes in front of the forehead.

④ When keeping the palm in becomes difficult, just move naturally. Keep the circle smooth and round.

The palms face up.

⑤ The tips of the middle fingers meet.

magnified view

now inhale
(after completing the movement)

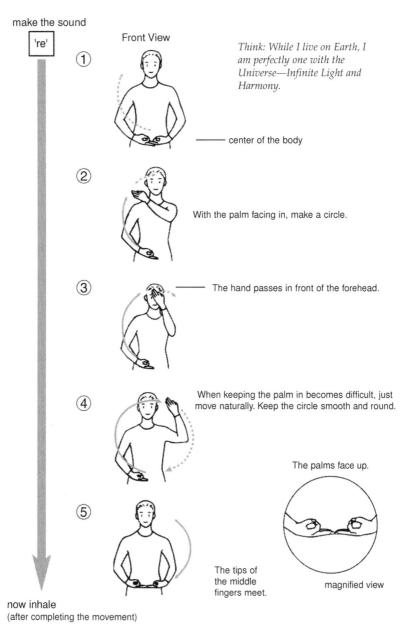

7 While making the sound 'so,' extend the right hand upward to the left. Turn the upper body in that direction. Then bring the hand back and place it by the right hip.

make the sound

'so'

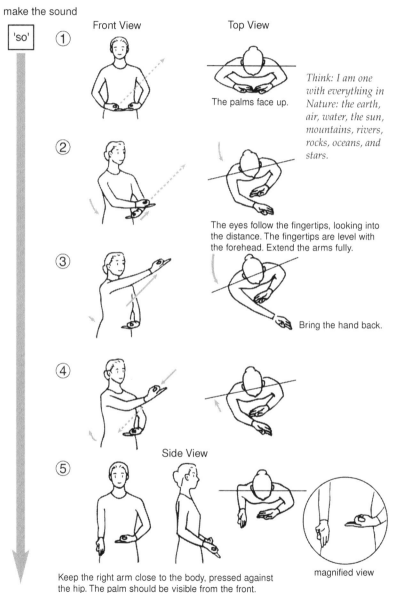

Front View

Top View

① The palms face up.

Think: I am one with everything in Nature: the earth, air, water, the sun, mountains, rivers, rocks, oceans, and stars.

②

The eyes follow the fingertips, looking into the distance. The fingertips are level with the forehead. Extend the arms fully.

③

Bring the hand back.

④

Side View

⑤

Keep the right arm close to the body, pressed against the hip. The palm should be visible from the front.

magnified view

now inhale
(after completing the movement)

147

8 While making the sound 'ku,' extend the left hand upward to the right. Turn the body in that direction. Then bring the hand back and place it by the left hip.

make the sound

'ku'

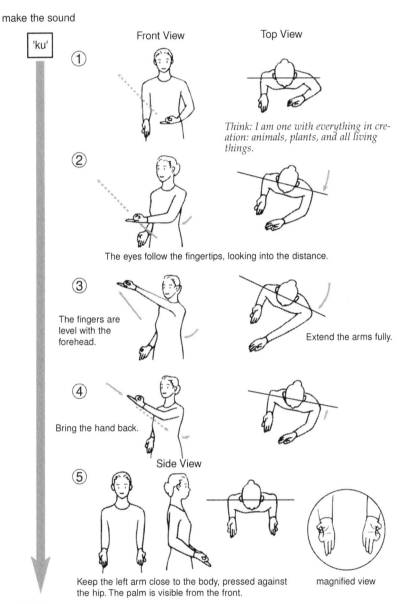

Front View

Top View

① Think: I am one with everything in creation: animals, plants, and all living things.

② The eyes follow the fingertips, looking into the distance.

③ The fingers are level with the forehead.

Extend the arms fully.

④ Bring the hand back.

Side View

⑤ Keep the left arm close to the body, pressed against the hip. The palm is visible from the front.

magnified view

now inhale
(after completing the movement)

148

9

While making the sound 'ka,' raise the right hand, fingers pointing up, palm to the front. At the same time, extend the left hand forward horizontally at the level of the chest.

make the sound

'ka'

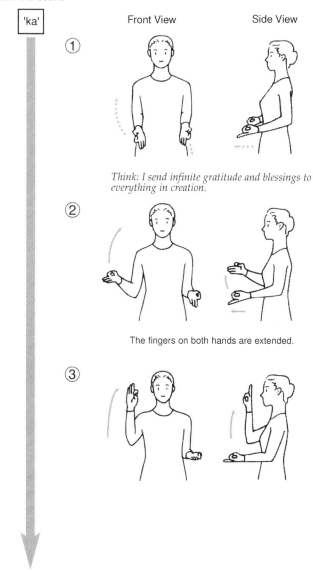

Front View Side View

①

Think: I send infinite gratitude and blessings to everything in creation.

②

The fingers on both hands are extended.

③

now inhale
(after completing the movement)

10 While making the sound 'mi,' reverse hand positions by bringing the left hand up and extending the right hand horizontally. Next, lower the left hand and bring the fingertips of both hands together in front of the body.

make the sound

'mi'

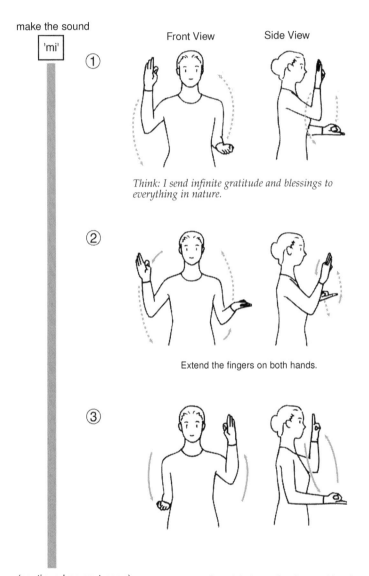

① Front View   Side View

Think: I send infinite gratitude and blessings to everything in nature.

② Extend the fingers on both hands.

③

(continued on next page)   Don't inhale yet. Continue making the sound 'mi.'

(continued from the previous page)

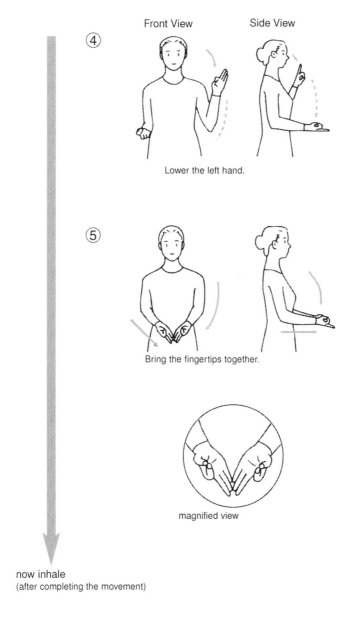

Front View   Side View

④

Lower the left hand.

⑤

Bring the fingertips together.

magnified view

now inhale
(after completing the movement)

11 While making the sound 'na,' raise both hands as if scooping something up. In front of the face, link the circles made by the forefingers and thumbs and press the palms and fingers together.

make the sound

'na'   Front View   Side View

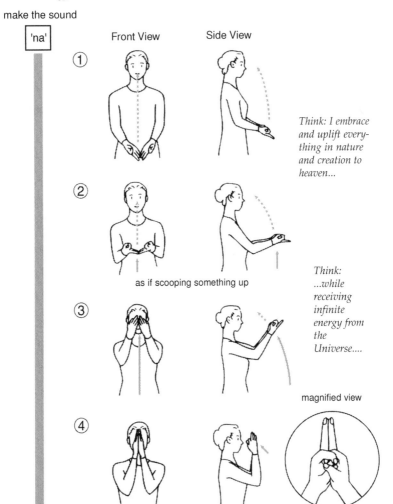

① Think: I embrace and uplift every-thing in nature and creation to heaven...

② as if scooping something up

Think: ...while receiving infinite energy from the Universe....

③ magnified view

④ Link the circles and press the palms and fingers together.

Either the right or left thumb can be in front of the other. Press the palms together as much as possible.

now inhale
(after completing the movement)

12 While making the sound 'ri,' separate the hands and lower them to hip level.

make the sound

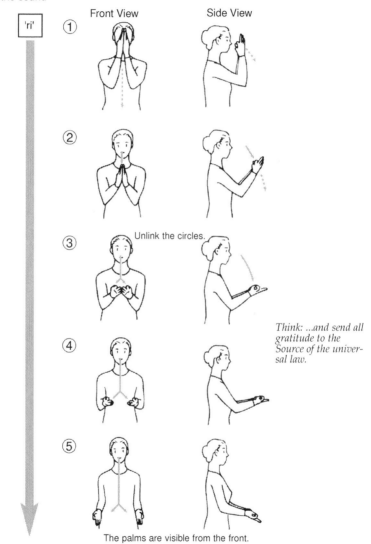

'ri'

Front View   Side View

①

②

③ Unlink the circles.

Think: ...and send all gratitude to the Source of the universal law.

④

⑤

The palms are visible from the front.

now inhale
(after completing the movement)

13 Holding the breath and leaving the left hand as it is, extend the forefinger on the right hand. From the middle of the body, thrust the right finger straight down, and raise it until it is level with the forehead.

no sound
(hold your breath)

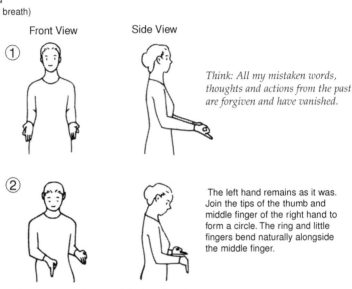

Front View   Side View

①

Think: All my mistaken words, thoughts and actions from the past are forgiven and have vanished.

②

The left hand remains as it was. Join the tips of the thumb and middle finger of the right hand to form a circle. The ring and little fingers bend naturally alongside the middle finger.

Point the index finger straight down from the middle of the body. The palm faces left.

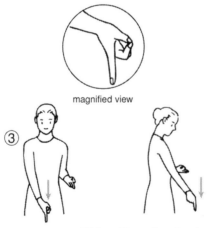

magnified view

③

While making a silent shout in you mind and body, thrust your right hand straight down.

(continued from the previous page)

Front View   Side View

④

After thrusting the hand down, without relaxing concentration, turn the finger straight upwards. Lift the finger slowly.

⑤

When the hand passes in front of the chest, thrust the finger upwards quickly. At the same time, again emit a silent shout in your mind and body.

Bring the hand down in front of the face and stop briefly.

⑥

Think: my infinite self has appeared.

Don't inhale yet.

14 Without losing concentration, lower the hands to the starting position and form the In of Great Harmony. Now release the breath.

now inhale
(after completing the movement)

How to Form the
Universal IN for Humanity

Before you start, say: *Jin-rui-so-ku-ka-mi-na-ri*
(Humanity is one with the Universe)

1 Starting position: The *IN* of Great Harmony

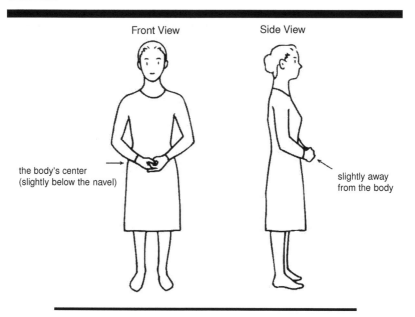

Front View   Side View

the body's center
(slightly below the navel)

slightly away
from the body

How to form the *IN* of Great Harmony

1. Make circles by joining the tips of the forefingers and thumbs.

2. Link the circles together.

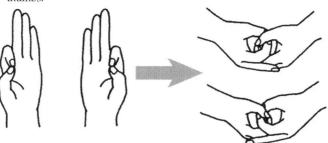

The palms face up.
Either hand can be on top.

2 After forming the *IN* of Great Harmony, release the linked circles as you lift the hands upward towards heaven from the body's center. With the hands touching each other as in the magnified view, raise them upwards in a gentle, curving motion until they are slightly above eye level. Relax your elbows. Don't over extend your arms.

make the sound

'uu'

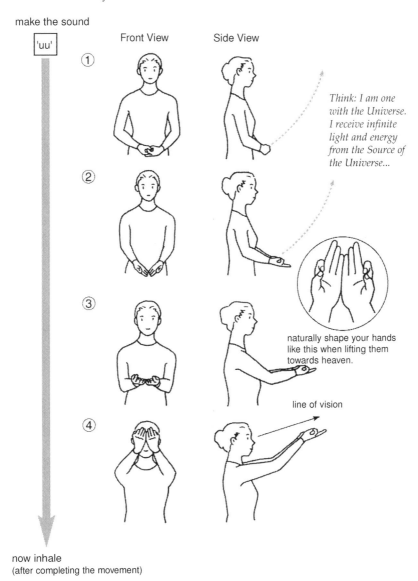

Front View   Side View

① ② ③ ④

Think: I am one with the Universe. I receive infinite light and energy from the Source of the Universe...

naturally shape your hands like this when lifting them towards heaven.

line of vision

now inhale
(after completing the movement)

While making the sound 'uu,' and without moving your left hand, move your right hand upward to a vertical position. Make sure the wrists are constantly touching each other.

make the sound

'uu'

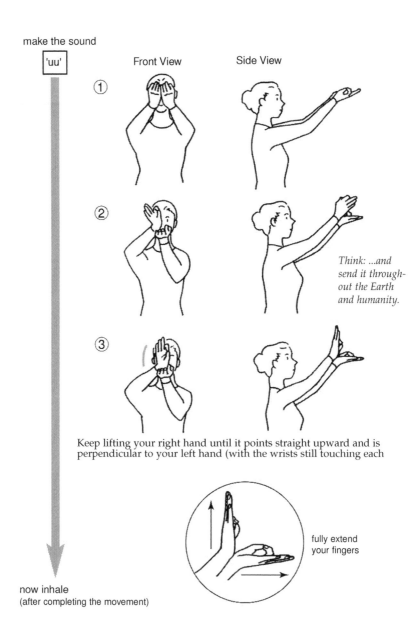

Front View   Side View

①

②

Think: ...and send it throughout the Earth and humanity.

③

Keep lifting your right hand until it points straight upward and is perpendicular to your left hand (with the wrists still touching each

fully extend your fingers

now inhale
(after completing the movement)

158

While making the sound 'ji,' and leaving your left hand as it is, bring the right hand up in a circular motion, forming a circle slightly larger than your face. The right hand moves clockwise and returns full circle.

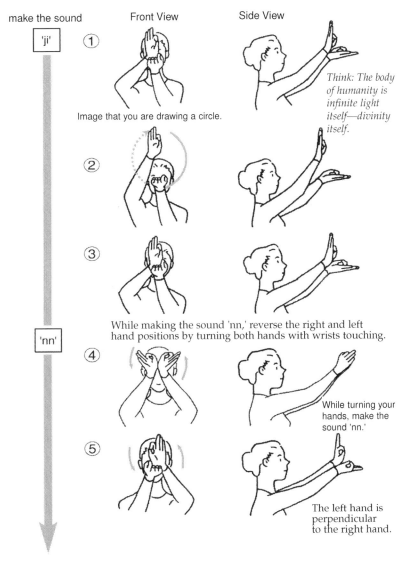

make the sound

'ji'

Front View

Side View

① Image that you are drawing a circle.

Think: The body of humanity is infinite light itself—divinity itself.

②

③

While making the sound 'nn,' reverse the right and left hand positions by turning both hands with wrists touching.

'nn'

④

While turning your hands, make the sound 'nn.'

⑤

The left hand is perpendicular to the right hand.

now inhale
(after completing the movement)

Note: make the sound 'ji-nn' in one breath.

159

While making the sound 'ru', keep your right hand as it is and make a circular motion with your left hand, forming a circle that is slightly larger than your face, and returning full circle. (From your point of view the circle will be counterclockwise.)

make the sound

'ru'

Front View

Side View

Think: The spirit of humanity is infinite light itself—divinity itself.

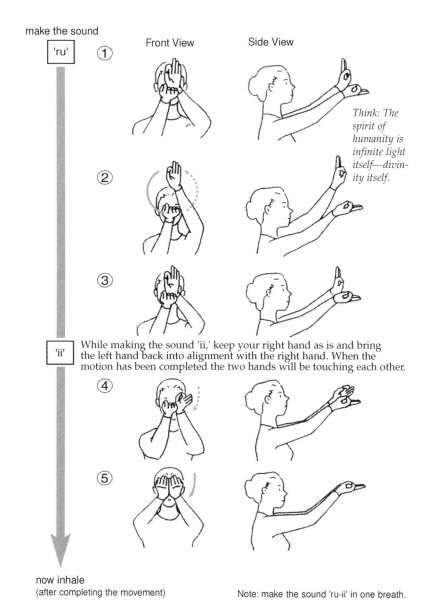

While making the sound 'ii,' keep your right hand as is and bring the left hand back into alignment with the right hand. When the motion has been completed the two hands will be touching each other.

'ii'

now inhale
(after completing the movement)

Note: make the sound 'ru-ii' in one breath.

While making the sound 'uu,' bring the right hand towards the left side of the chest and the left hand towards the right side of the chest, and cross your hands in front of you. The fingers extend upward toward heaven and the palms face out.

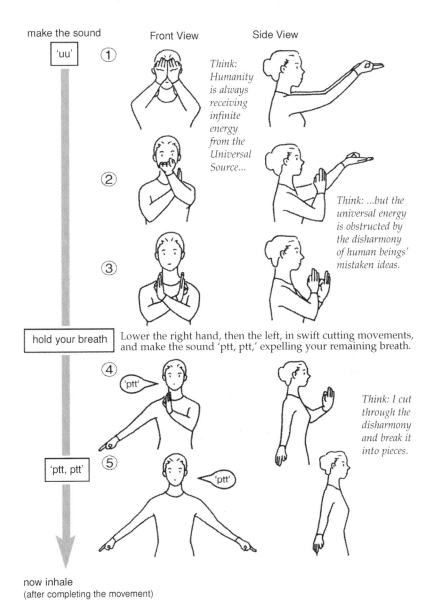

make the sound

'uu'

Front View   Side View

① *Think: Humanity is always receiving infinite energy from the Universal Source...*

② *Think: ...but the universal energy is obstructed by the disharmony of human beings' mistaken ideas.*

③

hold your breath   Lower the right hand, then the left, in swift cutting movements, and make the sound 'ptt, ptt,' expelling your remaining breath.

④ 'ptt'   *Think: I cut through the disharmony and break it into pieces.*

'ptt, ptt'   ⑤ 'ptt'

now inhale
(after completing the movement)

7 While making the sound 'so,' bring both arms up to shoulder level. Forming a wide arc, bring both hands in front of the chest. The tips of the middle fingers are touching. The palms face downward.

make the sound

'so'

Front View   Side View

Think: I calm the struggling movement of humanity's mistaken ideas and gather them together...

Top View

the hands meet in front of the chest

(continued on next page)

(continued from the previous page)

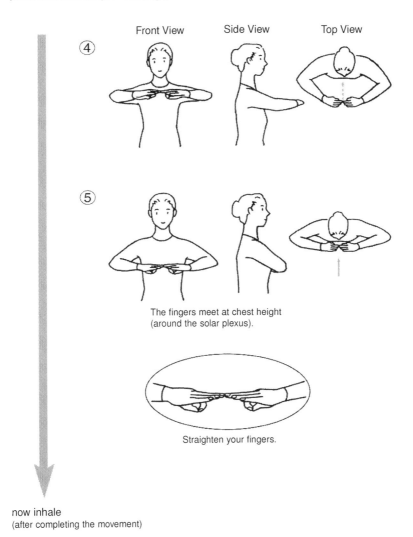

Front View   Side View   Top View

The fingers meet at chest height
(around the solar plexus).

Straighten your fingers.

now inhale
(after completing the movement)

163

8 While making the sound 'ku,' turn your palms up with your middle fingertips still touching. Extend your hands out in front of you, then spread them out widely to either side, palms still facing up. Gradually bring the hands down and cross them in front of the navel area, the right hand over the left.

make the sound

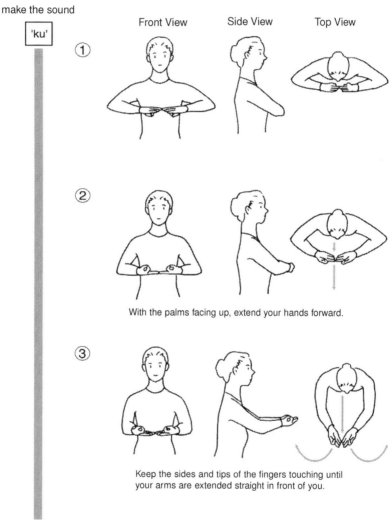

Front View   Side View   Top View

①

②

With the palms facing up, extend your hands forward.

③

Keep the sides and tips of the fingers touching until your arms are extended straight in front of you.

(continued on next page)

(continued from the previous page)

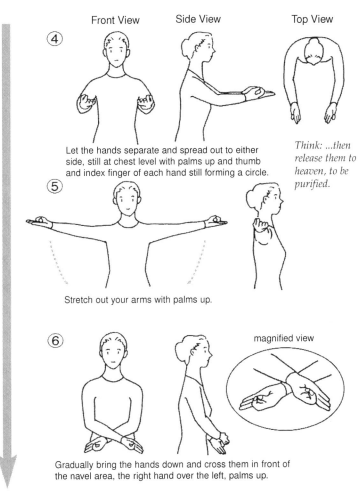

Front View   Side View   Top View

④

Let the hands separate and spread out to either side, still at chest level with palms up and thumb and index finger of each hand still forming a circle.

Think: ...then release them to heaven, to be purified.

⑤

Stretch out your arms with palms up.

⑥

magnified view

Gradually bring the hands down and cross them in front of the navel area, the right hand over the left, palms up.

now inhale
(after completing the movement)

While making the sound 'ka,' make a large, circular movement by lifting the arms upward on either side and crossing the hands above your head, palms facing inward with the inside of the left wrist touching the back of the right wrist. Continue the same sweeping, circular movement by bringing both hands downward in front of you and circling upward again until they extend straight out horizontally at either side (shoulder height, palms facing down).

make the sound

'ka'

Front View

Side View

① Think: Each human being is reborn as infinite light itself, infinite love itself...

② the big circle means infinity

line of vision

③ the palms face up

The palms face in. The right hand comes in front of the left.

(continued on next page)

166

(continued from the previous page)

Front View   Side View

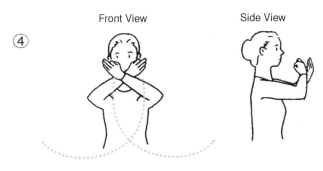

The right and left hands cross as
they move downward in a circling motion.

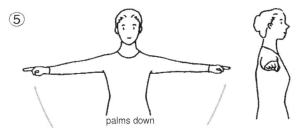

palms down

The arms sweep upward to either side, stopping at shoulder height.
The fingers extend straight out to the side, palms down.

now inhale
(after completing the movement)

167

10

While making the sound 'mi,' bring the hands downward in a circling movement. The hands cross in front of the navel area, the right hand under the left. As the hands cross, the palms of both hands turn outward. The circling movement continues until the hands cross above the head, with the inside of the left wrist brushing against the back of the right wrist. The circling movement continues downward until the arms extend straight outward to the sides at shoulder height, palms facing downward.

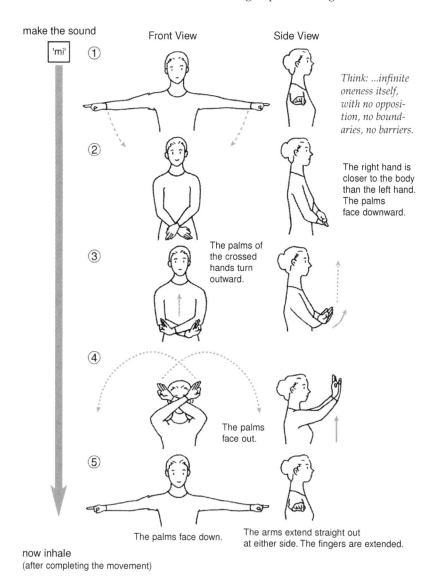

make the sound

'mi'

Front View

Side View

① *Think: ...infinite oneness itself, with no opposition, no boundaries, no barriers.*

② The right hand is closer to the body than the left hand. The palms face downward.

③ The palms of the crossed hands turn outward.

④ The palms face out.

⑤ The palms face down.　The arms extend straight out at either side. The fingers are extended.

now inhale
(after completing the movement)

168

11

While making the sound 'na,' lower your hands and bring them together in front of you. Then raise the hands as if scooping something up. When the hands are in front of the face, form circles made with the forefinger and thumb of each hand, and link the circles together. The palms and the fingers are pressed together.

make the sound

'na'

Front View   Side View

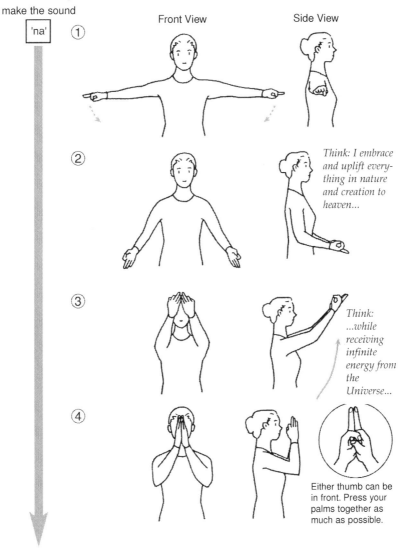

①

② Think: I embrace and uplift everything in nature and creation to heaven...

③ Think: ...while receiving infinite energy from the Universe...

④ Either thumb can be in front. Press your palms together as much as possible.

now inhale
(after completing the movement)

12 While making the sound 'ri,' separate the hands and lower them to hip level.

make the sound

'ri'

Front View   Side View

①

②

③

Think: ...and send all gratitude to the Source of the universal law.

④ unlink the circles

⑤

The palms are visible from the front.

now inhale
(after completing the movement)

13 While holding your breath, form a figure '7' (a crossed seven, as written in European countries) with your index finger.

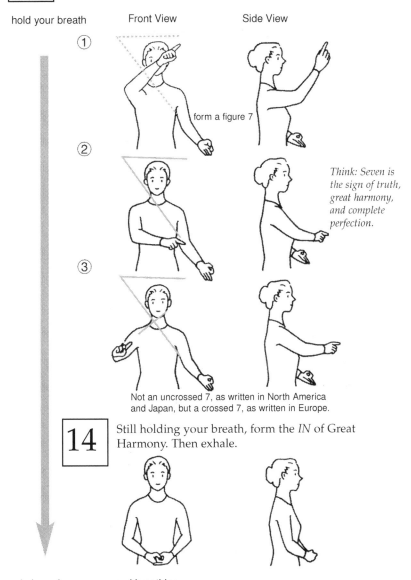

hold your breath

Front View Side View

① form a figure 7

② *Think: Seven is the sign of truth, great harmony, and complete perfection.*

③

Not an uncrossed 7, as written in North America and Japan, but a crossed 7, as written in Europe.

14 Still holding your breath, form the *IN* of Great Harmony. Then exhale.

exhale and resume normal breathing
(after completing the movement)

Interview with Masami Saionji
Questions and Answers
about Mandalas

*Recently, the practice of writing mandalas has been spreading to
people of all ages, faiths, and cultural backgrounds. In this special interview, Masami Saionji answers some questions about the
whys and hows of mandalas.*

Q: First, would you please explain what a mandala is?

A: A mandala might perhaps be thought of as a spiritual art
form. For hundreds of years, people of various faiths and cul-
tures have been creating mandalas to depict the divine truths
of the universe. Mandalas are usually round (the word mandala comes from the ancient Sanskrit word for circle), and can
be done in an endless variety of colors and media. For example, they can be painted, drawn, woven, pasted, or written
with words.

Until recently, mandalas were created only by special, holy
people. Nowadays, though, the practice of making mandalas
has become quite popular. This is because we are entering an

age when all human beings—not just a few—will be recognized as holy.

To me, a mandala is not only meant to be looked at. It is meant to be experienced. Writing a mandala is a step that a person takes in the evolution of his or her soul, and it simultaneously works for the evolution of humanity. I sincerely hope that in reading the following interview, even one person may be inspired to write his or her own original, joy-filled mandala.

Q: Next, would you please explain the principle behind the practice of writing mandalas?

A: The universe is constantly evolving and developing, and the universal source is constantly radiating its infinite energy everywhere. Infinite power, infinite wisdom, infinite richness, infinite brilliance, infinite capability, infinite expansiveness, and infinite creativity are constantly beaming down on us from our universal source.

Yet, this universal energy cannot manifest itself on the physical plane just as it is. It must first combine with physical energy. Otherwise the universal energy, in and of itself, cannot create anything new. It only keeps radiating, never manifesting itself, never taking shape.

That is why the universal energy wants to make contact with physical vessels, or instruments, that can merge with it and give expression to it in this world of creation.

There are various kinds of 'vessels' or 'instruments' that can merge with the sublime, ultimate light and energy of the universal source. The first of these is the physical body. Another vessel is the physical voice. Still others could be land, or water, or anything else that has life.

'Life' actually means 'God.' Life is God, and God is life. Everything that has life is a divine manifestation. Land, water, air, and everything in nature are alive, and give expression to the divine. That is why we honor, respect, and feel gratitude toward everything in the world of nature.

At present, there are about six billion people in this world, and all of them are capable of connecting with the infinite energy radiating from the universal source. At this time, however, most people do not know how to make this connection. That's why the universal energy is always searching for a connecting point which it can pass through and then spread out in the physical plane.

When I say 'connecting point,' I mean something that can function like a lens. Through this kind of 'lens' or 'instrument,' the universal energy can converge and then spread out widely, manifesting its principles of peace and harmony in this physical plane.

The divine, universal energy will work through any kind of instrument, any kind of vessel that is available to it. It can work through *INs*, or mandalas, or the voice, or the body, or prayer, or light—the possibilities are endless. Any kind of instrument can make contact with the source of the universal law. And the method for connecting with it depends on what kind of substance it is.

When I say 'substance,' I mean 'resonance.' Every vessel has its own unique resonance. Prayer has a resonance. Land has a resonance. Our physical elements also have a resonance. The universal energy can work though any substance or resonance that is capable of receiving it.

When you have a high awareness of this principle, you can create your own substance, your own instrument for connecting with the universal law. This will make it much easier for you to bring down the universal energy and let it become active in this physical plane.

In my case, I was able to uplift my awareness by communing with Goi Sensei through prayer. While I was in Europe in 1993 and 1994, after praying special prayers for eight hours every day for two years, I became able to bring down one aspect of the universal law in the form of the Universal *IN*. Everyone is capable of bringing down an aspect of the universal law, in their own unique way, when they attune themselves with the movement of the universal law.

Actually, the ways of manifesting the universal law are unlimited. There are no fixed rules for it. The universal law never says 'You must communicate with me only through *INs*, or only through mandalas, or only by going to the mountains, or only by burying some special words in the ground, and no other method will do!' If that were the case, how would it be possible for people without the use of their hands to connect with the universal law? How would it be possible for people without the use of their eyes or their feet to become one with the infinite energy of the universe? The method depends on the person. It depends on what kind of vibrations the person has, along with their age, and a variety of other factors. Everyone is capable of creating their own way of connecting with the universal divine law.

At this time, however, most people do not clearly know how to create a method for connecting with the universal law. That is why, for the time being, I am inviting everyone to try the methods that I and others like me have been using.

Q: Do you mean methods like INs, mandalas, gratitude to nature, bright thinking, and prayers for world peace?

A: Yes. Actually, to copy the excellent methods that other people have used can be a marvelous experience. Think about the great artists of recent centuries: Cezanne, Van Gogh, the impressionists, and so on. Before they developed their own style, all of them had the experience of copying the works of the great artists who had lived before them.

The same is true for *INs* and mandalas. I first brought down the *INs* and mandalas from within the universal law, and after that, a lot of people adopted or 'copied' those practices. And as those people were creating their mandalas or doing their *INs*, they each began to discern their own unique path and their own unique way of doing things. Feelings like 'I want to do this!' or 'I want to try that!' spontaneously began to surge up from within them. In this way, each person began to envision a simpler or a more powerful method of their own.

We can compare this with the creativity of artists. For example, Renoir, Cezanne, and Van Gogh were all very good painters, but who can say which was the greatest or which is most worth learning from? That depends on you. If you want to experience the beauty of Renoir's use of color, you can copy the works of Renoir. If you want to experience the subtlety of Cezanne's colors, you can copy the works of Cezanne. If you want to experience the vividness of Van Gogh's colors, you can copy the works of Van Gogh. And through that experience, you can communicate more deeply with the creative power within you—the power that tells you 'I want to do this!' or 'I want to try that!'

All great paintings have their own power, and the people

who see them are inspired and enlivened by them. Paintings have power, and so do mandalas.

Q: Would you say that copying is communication?

A: Yes, exactly. When you copy something that is vibrant with life, what you are really doing is communicating with it. When you copy a wonderful painting, you commune with it and exchange energy with it. You experience its spiritual power. By deeply encountering someone else's creation, you stir and awaken the creative power that you hold within yourself.

And of course, it is important to choose a work that speaks to you or holds the promise of something that you are longing for. It might be something that strikes a familiar note in you, or it might be something that appeals to you as being wonderfully different and new. Then, the experience of encountering and re-creating that divine work of art deepens and enriches you, and helps you to draw out your own marvelous talent.

When I was young, I used to wonder why art students had to copy others' work. But now I really find a deep meaning in it. Copying is communication. When artists copy, they can feel the communication. That's why they need to copy something that they truly admire and love.

Even though many other artists may have copied the same work, your re-creation of it will be different from anyone else's. If a hundred people copy a work by da Vinci, each of those hundred copies will have its own unique character. That's because each artist's talents are unique, and each communicates with da Vinci's work in a different way. Through their energy, their feelings, and their experiences from past lifetimes, each of them creates something unlike anyone else's. It is impossible for any two of them to create exactly the same copy. Each of them has their own unique sense of how to draw and how to express the painting's divine message.

Q: You often stress the importance of spending at least a little time with other people, to communicate with them and exchange energy with them...

A: That's right. It's very important to talk and communicate. Nowadays, a lot of young people have trouble communicating with each other, and this kind of isolation can lead to disastrous results—killing and all sorts of abuses. When people cut themselves off from others, they can lose their sense of the oneness of life. Nowadays, there is a growing tendency for people to communicate only through machines, but that is very dangerous.

Q: What kinds of communication would you say are most valuable?

A: All kinds of communication are valuable—communication through talking with people, through attuning ourselves to nature, and also through mandalas and various artistic creations. And whatever the medium is, whether it's painting, or sculpture, or flower arrangement, or jewelry, or clothing, or whatever it is, it has to be compatible with our personality and our state of mind. We have to like it and respect it. That's the basis for communication—respect, affinity, and gratitude. And as we keep developing our own awareness and our own means of communication and expression, we eventually create wonderful vessels that can connect with the source of the universal law.

Through our world peace prayers, *INs*, and mandalas, many of us have had experiences of connecting directly with the universal law. Also, when we pray together once a month at the sacred spot called Fuji Sanctuary,[16] we commune with one ray of light from the source of the universal law.

Under normal circumstances, it is unthinkable for the universal law, or universal light, to make direct contact with the third dimensional world. Because of its infinitely subtle vibrations, the ultimate energy of the universe can only reach as far as the spiritual (fourth dimensional) world. However, when several thousand people pray together for world peace at the same time and place, it becomes possible for one single ray of energy from the universal law to come through.

For all of the six billion people on Earth to join together and take the same form of divine expression would be, I think, too much to ask. But for ten or twenty thousand people, it is possible. Through their world peace prayers, *INs*, and mandalas, the people who pray together at Fuji Sanctuary already understand how to create their own vessels for the universal law. In the future, each of the six billion people on Earth will be able to create their own unique way, but for now, the best we can do is to appeal to the people who feel an affinity for our methods and wish to experience them.

Q: Since not everyone knows about mandalas, would you please start by letting our readers know what a mandala looks like?

A: The mandalas that we have been making are round, and they are made of bright, wonderful words that are capable of merging with the fundamental energy of the universe.

Q: How do we make a mandala?

A: First, we make an outline consisting of many concentric circles that get uniformly larger (see illustration). The total number of circles has to be a multiple of seven, because the number seven denotes completion. From the centermost point of the mandala, we draw a line that extends straight upwards to the outer edge of the biggest circle.

We begin to write from the centermost circle, forming our first letter right on top of the line. We write in the direction of the language (clockwise for English, counterclockwise for Hebrew, Arabic, and so on). When we have completed the first little circle, we continue from the next circle, always starting right on the line (see illustration).

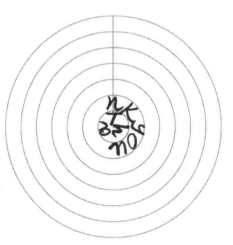

We continue writing until all the circles have been filled. As we near the end of the outermost circle, we gauge the remaining space to make sure that our final word sequence can fit precisely into the space remaining on the paper.

Q: What do we write in the rings?

A: That depends on what kind of mandala we are writing. If it is a Universal Source Mandala, we write the syllables *'wa-re-so-*

ku-ka-mi-na-ri' or *'jin-rui-so-ku-ka-mi-na-ri,'* which mean 'I am the Universe' and 'Humanity is the Universe,' respectively. If people want to write a Universal Source Mandala, there are some special procedures that need to be followed, so they will have to get in touch with my staff before they get started.

On the other hand, if they want to write a Mandala of Infinite Light or a Mandala of Gratitude to Nature, they can start right away.

Q: What is a Mandala of Infinite Light?

A: A Mandala of Infinite Light is made up of light-filled words or phrases. Many people like to make phrases starting with the word 'infinite.' For example, 'infinite light,' 'infinite harmony,' 'infinite peace,' and so on. You can make up your own phrases if you like, or you can refer to a list (see Appendix II). You can use the same word combination over and over again, or you can use a variety of words. You can create a pattern of colors, or you can use just one color.

If it is comfortable for you, I recommend that you try to hold your breath while you are writing. Just before you start writing, take in some air and hold it. You can write while you are holding your breath. Then, when you are ready to exhale, stop writing and resume your breathing. When you are ready to hold your breath again, continue writing from where you left off. However, if it puts a strain on you to hold your breath, you can write a Mandala of Infinite Light without holding your breath.

Q: What is the reason for holding our breath while we are writing?

A: When we hold our breath, the infinite light and energy of the universe become concentrated, and this allows greater power to flow into the words that we are writing.

It is important not to overstrain yourself, though. Day by day, you will develop a natural sense of how long you should hold your breath. When you are holding your breath properly, you will feel healthier and more alert. This is because your cells are being revitalized through the practice of holding your breath while focusing on light-filled words.

If, for any reason, you cannot seem to hold your breath at all, please don't worry about it. Just continue writing with sincerity and trust your body. Be guided by the wisdom of your body. Your body knows how to revive itself and how to support you best.

Q: Thank you. Next, would you please tell us about Mandalas of Gratitude to Nature?

A: Mandalas of Gratitude to Nature give us a wonderful way to honor various aspects of nature, such as the earth, the oceans, the mountains, minerals, plants, animals, the physical body, water, food, the air, the sun, the rain, the wind, the stars in the heavens, and so on.

When we make Mandalas of Gratitude to Nature, it is helpful to make a short declaration to the object of our gratitude on behalf of humanity. For example, if we want to write a mandala of gratitude to food, we can first say, 'On behalf of humanity, we thank you, dear food,' or something similar. The declaration can be long or short. If possible, we look at some food while we are speaking. A picture of food will suffice if there is no food nearby.

Q: Is it all right to write phrases of gratitude to many things in the same mandala—for example, to animals, vegetables, minerals, the earth, water, the mountains, and so on?

A: Yes, that is up to the person. You can write as many or as few expressions of gratitude as you wish in each mandala. You can make as many mandalas you wish—the more the better. The important thing is to write them with enjoyment, while drawing out your own sincere feelings of gratitude.

Q: What kinds of phrases do we write in a Mandala of Gratitude to Nature?

A: The choice of words is up to you. For example, if you are writing a mandala of gratitude to the earth, you could write 'beloved earth,' or 'noble earth,' or 'precious earth,' or 'thank you, dear earth,' or whatever words you prefer.

Q: What effects come from our writing Mandalas of Gratitude to Nature?

A: As you know, words are sources of power and energy. Words of gratitude are especially powerful, because gratitude is light itself. The light of gratitude can refresh and invigorate the weary, and heal all sorts of suffering.

For example, just imagine how you would feel if you were the Earth. People have been trampling on your body and causing painful explosions without caring at all about how it makes you feel. But when your body is infused with the light of gratitude, your strength revives, your suffering is lightened, and you can continue to provide love and support to humanity.

Mandalas of Gratitude to Nature send this kind of healing light and energy not only to the Earth, but to everything in nature—water, air, animals, trees and flowers, minerals, and so on. Everything in nature is suffering from the unfeeling behavior of human beings. Their energy fields have been tampered with and they are on the verge of collapsing.

Yet, if each person on Earth were to write a Mandala of Gratitude to Nature, I am certain that nature would revive and natural disasters would come to an end. Mandalas of Gratitude to Nature have that much power. Even one mandala will make a difference, so I urge everyone to write at least one if they feel a desire to.

Q: What effects come from our writing Mandalas of Infinite Light?

A: When we create a mandala using bright, positive words, we are creating ourselves. When I say 'creating ourselves,' I mean that we are imbuing ourselves with the qualities that we want most. We are calling those qualities forth from our universal source. We are instilling them in our consciousness, in our bodies, and in the atmosphere that we are projecting.

If you want to be a deeply loving person, you can write a mandala using words like 'infinite love.' If you want to be in harmony with others, you can write a mandala using words like 'harmony,' 'harmonized,' and 'harmonious.'[17] If you want to live more energetically, you can write a mandala with words like 'energy' and 'energetic.' Whatever divine qualities you long for, you can summon them from within the boundless universe and project them into your psychology and into your way of life by writing a Mandala of Infinite Light.

Q: Would you please give us a concrete idea of how this takes place?

A: A mandala works in a mystical way, through the world of vibrations. But I will try to explain the process as clearly as I can in terms of our present-day understandings.

A mandala functions something like a convex lens. As we are creating a mandala, we do experience its energy, but the full power is not activated until the entire mandala has been completed. Once the last word has been written and the last circle completed, the center of the mandala opens up to receive the energy of the universal source.

The process works like this. Universal energy flows in through all portions of the mandala, then comes together at the center. After coming together at the center, the energy flows back through the entire mandala, turning the mandala into an immense field of universal energy. Not only the written words, but also the paper that the words are written on is transformed into a powerful field of universal energy. From that time forward, the mandala becomes fully charged and it continues, at all times, to radiate its harmonizing energy through the physical plane.

A mandala of gratitude to the ocean, for example, is constantly at work, day and night, transmitting waves of gratitude to the ocean, dispelling the causes of tidal waves and other calamities. A mandala of gratitude to plants is constantly sending revitalizing energy to the ailing trees, flowers, and grasses. A mandala filled with words of infinite health and happiness is constantly emitting shining vibrations to us and to others, purifying our subconscious and transforming us into the bright, happy, healthy people that we wish to be.

Q: Why did the practice of creating our own mandalas emerge at this particular time?

A: That is because humanity as a whole is now on the verge of awakening to its inner truth. In earlier times, the majority of people did not believe in themselves enough to be able to create their own mandalas. If they knew about mandalas, they generally thought of them as something created by others—by saints and holy people—never by themselves. Now, however, as this planet continues to shift into a higher dimensional age—an age of spiritual civilization and culture—many people are changing. They are starting to sense their spiritual nature. They are starting to recognize themselves as creators. This allows them to conceive of creating their own mandalas.

Q: Next, would you please tell us about Universal Source Mandalas?

A: There are two kinds of Universal Source Mandalas. One kind expresses the universal nature of the individual who is writing the mandala. This kind is called a Mandala of *Wa-re-so-ku-ka-mi-na-ri. Wa-re-so-ku-ka-mi-na-ri* is a new term, a new *kotodama*[18] that descended from the world of the universal source. It means 'I am the Universe' or 'I am one with the Universe.'

The other kind expresses the divinity of humanity as a whole. These are called Mandalas of *Jin-rui-so-ku-ka-mi-na-ri. Jin-rui-so-ku-ka-mi-na-ri* is also a new *kotodama*, received from the universal source. Expressed in ordinary language, *jin-rui-so-ku-ka-mi-na-ri* would mean 'Humanity is the Universe' or 'Humanity is Divine.'

The process of writing a Universal Source Mandala is almost the same as for the other mandalas described above.

The main difference is that when we start writing a Universal Source Mandala, we need to register a ray of universal energy into the center of it.

When the practice of writing Universal Source Mandalas was conveyed to me from the source of the universal law, I was entrusted with a ray of universal energy to be registered in the center of each mandala. When the first group of people began writing their Universal Source Mandalas, two people (myself and the writer) registered the universal energy into the center through a clearly prescribed procedure. After completing his or her mandala, the person then became able to jointly register the light in other people's mandalas, in the same way as I do.

If our readers would like to write a Universal Source Mandala, they can contact me to find out more about it.

Q: Why are they called Universal Source Mandalas?

A: As you know, the syllables *wa-re-so-ku-ka-mi-na-ri* and *jin-rui-so-ku-ka-mi-na-ri* hold an essential vibration that allows our imagination to re-connect with the source of the universal law. Through this connection, special energy from the universal source fills our bodies and flows out into the mandala, creating a direct source of universal light and energy on Earth.

Q: You mentioned that when we write a Universal Source Mandala we must go through a special procedure to register the universal light in it. Yet, no such procedure is needed when we create Mandalas of Infinite Light or Mandalas of Gratitude to Nature. What is the reason for this?

A: The difference arises from the function of each kind of mandala. In the case of Mandalas of Infinite Light and Mandalas of Gratitude to Nature, an energy field for registering the light has already been firmly established in the vibrational world. As soon as anyone begins writing a Mandala of Infinite Light or a Mandala of Gratitude to Nature, the universal light instantly becomes registered in it.

But due to the special nature of a Universal Source Mandala, that kind of energy field has not yet been firmly established. That is why, at the present time, the light must be registered through our physical entities according to a precise procedure.

Q: What is the special nature of a Universal Source Mandala?

A: At the center of a Universal Source Mandala is the existence of the universal source itself. Through a Universal Source Mandala, the fundamental light of the universe resonates directly through the physical plane.

When we write a Universal Source Mandala, the original, mystical energy of the universe flows through our being and draws us back into the world of our source. Our Universal Source Mandala harmonizes the activity of our genes and focuses our consciousness on the center of our existence.

When we focus on the center of our existence, strife and confusion naturally fade away and we sense our original oneness with the universe. This enables us to advance along our own true path without getting sidetracked.

Q: Does a Universal Source Mandala also work like a lens, like the mandalas that you described before?

A: Yes, it does. As described earlier, the universal energy permeates the entire surface of the mandala, then converges at the center. From there, the concentrated energy flows out again to fill the entire mandala, as well as the paper that the mandala is written on. After that, it resonates outward through the three-dimensional plane.

In the case of a Mandala of *Wa-re-so-ku-ka-mi-na-ri*, the universal energy resonates from the mandala to the person who wrote the mandala, and it also reaches other people whose life vibrations, character, and personality resemble those of the writer. In the case of a Mandala of *Jin-rui-so-ku-ka-mi-na-ri*, the universal energy resonates from the mandala to the writer and to each individual member of humanity.

As soon as a Universal Source Mandala has been completed, the energy of the universal source continues unceasingly to flow into it and then to spread out through the physical plane. This flow of universal energy continues endlessly.

Q: Is there any danger of the mandala's resonance being too strong?

A: No. The mandala has its own flawless wisdom, and it sends out just the quantity of energy that the individual (or humanity) requires and is able to accept. If we need gentle energy, it provides us with gentle energy. Depending on how we change and develop, our mandala adjusts the amount of energy that it sends to us.

Q: After we finish writing our mandalas, what should we do with them?

A: Your mandalas are your priceless treasures, and they

deserve to be treated with love and respect. Unless they are unusually big, they can be framed and hung on the wall as sources of light and inspiration. Small mandalas can be carried with you on trips or kept at your workplace.

Q: Is there any charge involved in writing a mandala?

A: Only for the materials, if people choose to obtain preprinted mandala forms. But they are free to create their own forms if they wish. In that case, it will not cost them anything.

It is not permissible to charge money for assisting people in writing mandalas or for registering the universal energy in them.

Q: Can sightless people make mandalas?

A: Yes. They have been using forms where the circles stand out in relief, so that they can feel the lines with their hands. The mandalas they have made are really marvelous.

Anyone who wants to write a mandala can find their own way of doing it. The important thing, I feel, is for people to follow their inner voice and do their best to draw out their own creativity in their own way. It depends on what you, yourself, really want to do.

Every situation is different. Every person is different. Every person is free to choose his or her own way of connecting with the universal law. Nothing is firmly fixed to begin with. Everything is changing and evolving. Just as the laws that govern the workings of the universe are changing and evolving, each person's creativity is also changing and evolving.

Creativity starts within the mind. Everyone is capable of

creating an image within their mind, and of drawing it out into the world of reality.

Q: Have you any final words for our readers?

A: Yes. Just reading about mandalas cannot give you the experience of creating one—and it is an experience that I recommend highly. If you wish to write a mandala, it means that your mandala is waiting to be written. It wants to communicate with you and send you its love and guidance.

If there is anything I can do to enable even one more person to create a mandala, it will be a great pleasure for me to help. Please do not hesitate to get in touch with me.

On behalf of our readers, thank you very much for this valuable interview.

Please note: Readers who are interested in learning more about mandalas and creating their own mandalas may download blank mandala forms from the website http://www.earthhealershandbook.net. Choose 'Mandala Workbook' from the main menu, and scroll to the bottom to download and print the forms.

A New, Quick, and Effective Method

In January 2003, a new spiritualized breathing method was introduced by Masami Saionji, and it is gaining wide recognition as wonderful way to purify ourselves and enhance our creativity. Everyone is welcome to use it!

This method has the following three steps:

1. Inhale deeply while thinking: *wa-re-so-ku-ka-mi-na-ri* ('I am one with the Universe').

2. Before exhaling, pause for a few seconds while silently making a positive declaration to yourself, such as 'It will definitely go well!' or 'It's absolutely all right!' Or, you can simply think, 'Accomplished!'

3. Quietly and calmly, exhale through the mouth while thinking: *jin-rui-so-ku-ka-mi-na-ri* ('Humanity is one with the Universe').

At the moment of birth, we human beings naturally begin to breathe with our own power. Each time we breathe, we receive life-giving energy and spiritual elements from the universe. At the moment of death, we exhale our last breath and return to our universal source. Birth and death are closely related to our breathing, and it is through our breathing that we continually purify and heal ourselves.

However, with the development of material culture and civilization, most of us have forgotten how to breathe properly. As a result, we have lost much of our self-purification power. This new method works to reverse that tendency.

By deeply inhaling while thinking *'wa-re-so-ku-ka-mi-na-ri,'* we receive pure, light-filled energy from the world of the universal source. This energy travels through the cerebral cortex and is carried to all our organs and bodily functions via the blood and the nervous system.

As we inhale, the sounds *'wa-re-so-ku-ka-mi-na-ri'* resonate through the universe, attracting divine life elements which are taken into the body. Then, as we briefly hold our breath while thinking a positive thought, the life-energy we have inhaled communicates with all the cells of our body, purifying poisonous elements. At the same time, the creative power of the universe is exerted. Finally, by thinking *'jin-rui-so-ku-ka-mi-na-ri'* as we exhale, we resonate truth and harmony to all human beings.

As we continue to practice this method, our health and our character naturally improve, and our future takes a turn for the better. Even people who once thought of themselves as weak-willed can discover that they are now freely giving expression to their own positive will.

If you would like to share your experiences with this method or ask any questions about it, please refer to the author's contact information on page 197.

Notes

1. The essential meaning of *karma* is 'work.' It is the work, or creativity, of our thought waves. In this book, terms like 'karma' or 'karmic' refer mainly to negative kinds of karma. Here, it refers to the destructive energy that has built up through many centuries of unharmonious thinking.

2. In this book, the word 'truth' generally refers to higher truths, such as principles of harmony, divine love, and the oneness of life. It could also be thought of as the truth of our intrinsic nature as human beings.

3. 'Sakyamuni Buddha' refers to the saint whose teachings formed the basis of Buddhism. The spelling 'Shakamuni' is also commonly used.

4. An *IN* is a method for attuning ourselves with the universal laws of harmony. Details are given in Appendix IV.

5. Cosmic science is a harmonized science issuing from higher dimensional planes. More information about cosmic science will be available at a future date.

6. The phrase 'May peace prevail on Earth' is used in the author's teachings and was created by her adoptive father, Masahisa Goi. Details are given in Appendix I. The other phrases are examples of what the author refers to as 'bright thinking.' Details are given in Appendix II.

7. This refers to a ceremony held at a place called Fuji Sanctuary in Shizuoka, Japan on July 24, 1994.

8. This is believed to refer to the *IN* which was introduced at the above mentioned July 24 ceremony. Please see Appendix IV.

9. For more examples of bright thoughts, please see Appendix II.

10. Masahisa Goi, *The Spirit of Lao Tsu*, Byakko Press, 2001.

11. Please refer to Appendix III to practice expressing gratitude to nature.

12. Instead of saying, 'I am one with the Universe,' readers may wish to use the international sounds *'wa-re-so-ku-ka-mi-na-ri.'* These sounds convey the meaning 'I am a universal divine being,' and can be incorporated into any language.

13. For information about mandalas, please refer to Appendix VI.

14. This concept is conveyed in the Biblical passage: *In the beginning was the Word, and the Word was with God, and the Word was God* (John 1:1). 'The Word' refers to divine vibrations, or

waves of light, which create everything in the universe. The same concept is also taught in the Shinto faith, where it is called *kotodama*, or 'word-spirit,' the divine energy of a word before it enters the world of human thought waves. *Kotodamas* are discussed further in Appendix VI.

15. This refers to Masahisa Goi, the adoptive father and mentor of Masami Saionji. *Sensei* is the Japanese word for 'teacher.'

16. Fuji Sanctuary is a peace center located in Shizuoka, Japan.

17. Recently, Ms. Saionji has been encouraging people to write mandalas combining positive words with their own names. For example: 'Beloved Jane Smith,' 'Purified Andrew Jones,' and so on.

18. *Kotodama* refers to the original, divine spirit of a word, before it enters the world of thought waves.

About the Author

Masami Saionji is descended from the Royal Ryukyu Family of Okinawa. Educated in Japan and the United States, she is known internationally as the leader of the world peace prayer movement initiated by her adoptive father, Masahisa Goi. She has authored sixteen books in Japanese and five in English and other languages. She and her husband, the descendent of a Japanese prime minister, have three daughters. They currently live in Tokyo.

In November 2001, Ms. Saionji was named an honorary member of the Club of Budapest in recognition of her exceptional efforts for world peace.

To contact the author, or for more information about any of the subjects discussed in *You Are the Universe*, please write to:

Masami Saionji
c/o Infinity 21
Minato-ku, Akasaka 1-1-7-1102
Tokyo, Japan 107-0052

Fax: +81-(0)3-5411-2710

E-mail: info@thinksomethingwonderful.net

Made in the USA
San Bernardino, CA
10 March 2017